SLOW COOKER

COOKER

CENTRAL

Family Favourites

SLOW
COOKER
CENTRAL

Family Favourites

Paulene Christie

ABC
BOOKS

The ABC 'Wave' device is a trademark of the
Australian Broadcasting Corporation and is used
under licence by HarperCollins*Publishers* Australia.

First published in Australia in 2019
by HarperCollins*Publishers* Australia Pty Limited
ABN 36 009 913 517
harpercollins.com.au

Some recipes in this book were previously published in *Slow Cooker Central*,
Slow Cooker Central 2, *Slow Cooker Central: Super Savers* and *Slow Cooker Central: Kids*.

HarperCollins*Publishers*
Level 13, 201 Elizabeth Street, Sydney, NSW 2000, Australia
Unit D1, 63 Apollo Drive, Rosedale, Auckland 0632, New Zealand
A 53, Sector 57, Noida, UP, India
1 London Bridge Street, London, SE1 9GF, United Kingdom
Bay Adelaide Centre, East Tower, 22 Adelaide Street West, 41st Floor, Toronto,
  Ontario, M5H 4E3, Canada
195 Broadway, New York, NY 10007, USA

A catalogue record for this book is available
from the National Library of Australia

ISBN: 978 0 7333 3923 3 (paperback)
ISBN: 978 1 4607 0959 7 (ebook)

Cover design by Gemma Banks, HarperCollins Design Studio
Cover images by shutterstock.com
Author photo by Karlie Holloway
Typeset by Kirby Jones
Printed and bound in Australia by McPherson's Printing Group
The papers used by HarperCollins in the manufacture of this book are a natural, recyclable product
made from wood grown in sustainable plantation forests. The fibre source and manufacturing
processes meet recognised international environmental standards, and carry certification.

Dedicated to Simon and Caleb, Talyn & Ella
My people
My today, my tomorrow and my always
Xx

Contents

Introduction 1

Slow Cooker Hints & Tips 3

Soups 29

Pasta 41

Vegetables 53

International Flavours 77

Lamb 99

Chicken 111

Sausages 151

Beef 167

Seafood 185

Pork 197

Mince & Meatballs 215

Eggs & Breakfast 239

Desserts, Cakes & Sweets 249

Breads, Dips & Sauces 273

Index 281

Acknowledgements 293

INTRODUCTION

Welcome to the newest book in the Slow Cooker Central series ... *Family Favourites*. It doesn't feel like that long ago that I was writing the introduction for our last book, or for the books before that, yet here we are at book five! What a wild ride it's been – first let me take you back on the journey that led us to this point ...

In 2012 I launched our Facebook group 'Slow Cooker Recipes 4 Families'. I had hoped a few of my friends may join me in my interest in slow cooking and perhaps we could share some recipes and ideas. Little did I know that the group would grow to be a global hit with over half a million members from all over the world in just a few short years. We soon had to create the www.slowcookercentral. com website to adequately showcase and archive our thousands of recipes, our slow cooker blog articles and our many slow cooker reviews.

In 2014 we were approached by the amazing team at ABC Books and HarperCollins Australia and asked to create and release a book to share the recipes of our community! In 2015 we released that first book in our series, *Slow Cooker Central*. Soon followed by *Slow Cooker Central 2* the following year in 2016. In 2017 our newest edition, *Slow Cooker Central Super Savers* took a budget focus, gathering recipes that ranged from $5 to $25 each to suit all budgets. 2018 saw the release of *Slow Cooker Central Kids*, recipes that all families, but especially the kids, would love to eat and could also help us to cook.

All these books were a mix of my own recipes and those submitted by members of our community and every one of these books topped the Australian bestseller lists!

With this latest addition we have taken a new turn. *Slow Cooker Central Family Favourites* is a collection of recipes purely from my own kitchen. I've gathered a collection of 200 of my best recipes for you: 100 brand new and never-before seen recipes plus 100 of my most popular classics!

Recipes I've created for my family, that now your whole family can enjoy.

Recipes across all meal types, plus snacks, sweets and entertaining too!

Recipes cooked in my home kitchen, tested on the tastebuds of my willing family and friends, and perfected until I had them just right for you.

As always we stay true to our motto – real food, cooked by real people, in real kitchens! There are no exhaustive lists of fancy exotic ingredients no one has ever heard of. No complex steps or skills that require years of training in the kitchen to master. No overly styled or Photoshopped glossy photos that no one can hope to recreate.

Real food. Real results.

Food that's easy to prepare and delicious to eat!

I hope you and your family enjoy this collection of my Family Favourites From my kitchen to yours

Happy slow cooking everyone xx

Paulene Christie

SLOW COOKER
HINTS & TIPS

We have here what we hope is a great collection of tips and tricks and frequently asked questions that we have gathered from the collective experience in our slow cooking community.

We've covered some really important safety do's and don'ts to help you to get the very best out of your slow cooking experiments while minimising the risks that other cooks may unknowingly take. The section on the tea-towel trick helps explain what that strategy is all about – you will see it mentioned a lot in our recipes. It helps us make many of the unique and unusual dishes we create in our slow cookers.

So BEFORE you start cooking, have a read through the hints and tips that follow – and then your hardest decision after that will only be deciding which great recipe from the book to cook first.

Can I use frozen meat in the slow cooker?

This is a hotly debated topic. The short answer is yes, you *could*, but no – you should not! Many people will tell you they have done so for years and it's never hurt them. However, that's probably more to do with luck than anything else. Don't follow dangerous advice. It's a risk that is quite frankly unnecessary, and we hope is one that you won't take with yourself or those being served your meals. Here's why…

Health concerns

Although some people will state that they cook frozen meat in their slow cookers, the health and food technology experts say that for food safety reasons you should bring your food to temperatures of 60°C (140°F) or more as quickly as possible. Some people assume that cooking frozen meat in a slow cooker works the same way as with other methods, but they are not the same. Food cooked in the oven or on a stovetop heats up much faster than in a slow cooker. Cooking frozen meat in a slow cooker significantly increases the amount of time it takes for food to reach the safe temperature target, and thus significantly increases the chances of you and your family getting food poisoning.

Cooker care

Cooking meat from frozen also increases the risk of a ceramic slow cooker bowl cracking as a result of the wide difference in temperature between the frozen food and the heating bowl. If the bowl cracks, your slow cooker is unusable.

On a similar note, you should always remove the food from your slow cooker dish before refrigerating it. The nature of the thick ceramic bowl means it retains heat and thus takes a lot longer to cool down to safe refrigeration temperatures, once again leaving your food too long in the danger zone.

In Summary

Please don't prioritise convenience over safety. It may be that you have to take the time to defrost your meat first, or you may in fact have to change the meal you had planned to cook for today until tomorrow when you can have the meat defrosted – but it's worth it. I for one will not take that risk with my loved ones. You are free to weigh up this risk for you and your family and hopefully make the safe decision for your home. Cook smart – cook safe.

How can I thicken slow-cooker recipes with a high liquid content?

Slow cooking can produce dishes with excess liquid due to condensation forming on the lid and the fact the lid stays closed so the liquid doesn't reduce as with some stovetop or oven methods. Here's a collection of tips and trick you can use to ensure a thickened consistency to your final dish.

Cornflour (cornstarch)

Mix 1–2 tablespoons of cornflour with 1–2 tablespoons of cool tap water and mix until it becomes a thin runny paste without any lumps (some people prefer to use rice flour or arrowroot flour). Pour this mix straight into your slow cooker dish 20–30 minutes before serving and stir briefly around whatever is in the pot. Then leave the dish to continue cooking, preferably on HIGH but LOW if the recipe requires.

This added cornflour will thicken the liquids in the recipe. If this amount of cornflour doesn't thicken the liquids sufficiently, you can repeat the process. But take care not to add too much cornflour to your recipe – one or two additions are usually all that's needed. Some people ladle the liquid out of the slow cooker into a saucepan on the stove and add the cornflour there. How you do it is totally up to you.

Gravy granules/powder

Substitute gravy granules for cornflour and follow the method as described above. The suitability of this option will depend on the recipe and whether the addition of gravy will suit it.

Grated potato

Grate 1–2 raw potatoes and add them to the slow cooker 30–45 minutes before serving. Stir them as much as you can around the solid ingredients. This will very quickly thicken the dish and the remaining cooking time will allow the potato to cook through.

Grated potato will only suit some recipes – those with vegetable or potato already in them or which would be complemented by the addition of potato.

You can use instant potato flakes in place of grated raw potato.

Lift the lid

Another option is to remove the lid of the slow cooker or at least place it ajar for the last 30 minutes of cooking to enable the sauce to thicken through evaporation. This is not ideal as the very nature of the slow cooker is to provide a sealed environment to maintain the cooking temperature – but it is an option.

Use less liquid to begin with

A natural consequence of slow cooking is the increased moisture content thanks to the drip condensation from the lid down into the food during cooking. Many people think meat has to be covered in liquid to slow cook it, but in fact it needs very little liquid. If you find a dish is regularly ending up with far too much liquid, reduce the liquid in the initial recipe next time you cook it.

The tea towel trick

While the tea towel trick (see the next page) is normally used when slow cooking cakes and breads, it can be used to absorb some of the condensation from the dish when following non-baking recipes. Please read important safety information in the section regarding the tea towel trick.

Flour toss

Tossing your meat in flour before cooking can also thicken the dish.

Pulling/shredding

Pulling or shredding your meat at the end of the cooking time (assuming this suits the dish) will also take up a lot of the excess liquids in the pot.

The tea towel (dish towel) trick

Quite a few of the recipes in this book will ask you to 'Cook with a tea towel (dish towel) under the lid'. The tea towel, which lies between the top of the slow cooker bowl and the lid of the slow cooker, acts to absorb condensation and stop it from dripping down into the food cooking inside. It's often used when you wouldn't want the cake or bread being cooked ending up soggy.

Note that this method has been devised by home slow cooker enthusiasts and is not recommended officially or declared a safe practice by slow cooker manufacturers. Please carefully read the following information before deciding for yourself if it's something you wish to do.

When using the tea towel trick, regular users suggest you fold up any excess fabric from the towel up onto the lid of the slow cooker, securing it to the lid handle, so it doesn't hang down over the hot outer casing of the slow cooker – this is very important for safety! A tea towel on the lid absorbs liquid during the cooking process, so it stays somewhat damp and is unlikely to burn.

If you have concerns about the fire hazards related to this practice, you can research the safety issues involved and inform yourself about the pros and cons. It is totally up to you to appraise the risks and decide whether it is safe to use the tea towel method with your slow cooker.

It is not recommended to use the tea towel in general slow cooking, but just as an optional measure to reduce liquid in a dish. If you decide to use this technique, do so only for cakes, breads and baking or recipes where water dripping is a major issue.

Please make your own decision regarding the safety of this practice. If in any doubt, do not do this. I personally recommend you don't leave your home when you are using a tea towel in this way, so that you are able to keep an eye on your slow cooker and the towel.

How can I remove oil and fat from a slow cooker dish?

There are several methods you can use to remove oil from your dish. First and foremost, you can reduce the amount of fat going into the dish at the beginning.

Be choosy
Choose lean cuts of meat, trim visible fat from meat and add little to no oil to your slow cooker recipes.

Prep it
Pre-browning or sealing meat in a frying pan is one way to remove some of the fat before cooking it in the slow cooker (read more about pre-browning and sealing meat on pages 11–12).

Skim and discard
Perhaps the most obvious solution is to spoon that fat right out of there! Towards the end of the cooking process, the fat will often gather at the top of your dish so you can use a ladle or spoon to gently remove and discard it.

The ice-cube trick
Placing ice-cubes briefly on top of the dish will cause the fat to 'stick to' the ice-cubes (because the lower temperature causes the fat to solidify). You can then discard the ice-cubes and the oil right along with them.

The bread trick
Very briefly lay a piece of bread along the top of the dish. This will soak up the fat, which can be discarded with the bread or fed to a four-legged friend. But be very careful and always remove the bread with tongs, as it will be hot!

Some people use paper towel instead of bread to soak up the fats and oils, but if something is going to break down in my food, I would rather it were bread than paper.

Cool and skim
If you have the time or you are cooking a recipe in advance, you can cool the entire dish in the fridge overnight. The fat will solidify on top and you can remove it before reheating and serving the dish.

What does the AUTO function on my slow cooker do?

Many slow cookers have LOW, HIGH, KEEP WARM and AUTO settings. The AUTO function usually means the dish will begin cooking at HIGH for approximately 2 hours, then the slow cooker will switch itself down to the LOW temperature setting. (The dial itself doesn't move and will remain pointing to AUTO.)

This feature varies with different slow cooker models and brands, so always consult your user manual.

Are timers safe to use for slow cooking?

There is an important distinction between timers built in to a slow cooker and the wall kind that you plug into the power socket and then plug your slow cooker into.

A slow cooker with a timer function will generally switch your unit to a 'keep warm' mode after your pre-selected cooking time is complete. Most units will then only stay in this keep-warm mode for a limited number of hours for food safety reasons.

Wall timers are not recommended for slow cooking. For good reasons:

- Some people use them to delay the start time of cooking. This means the ingredients are sitting out, not cooking, for several hours before the slow cooker turns on. It's a recipe for a food-poisoning disaster.
- Some people use them to turn off the slow cooker at the end of the cooking time completely. This means your finished hot – and slowly getting cooler – dish is sitting out multiplying nasty bacteria in it until you get around to eating it. Again a recipe for a food-poisoning disaster. You would not cook a meal in your oven then just leave it in there or sitting on the kitchen bench for hours before eating it. A slow cooked meal is no different.

Definitely avoid timers designed for light fittings. These timers are not made to handle the load of a slow cooker. It could cause the slow cooker to burn out the element, or the timer itself could burn out or catch fire.

Cook smart, cook safe – please do not use wall timers for slow cooking.

Is it safe to leave my slow cooker unattended all day while I am out of the house?

In short, yes ... with precautions.

Slow cookers are designed to run all day unattended without posing a fire hazard. There are, however, further precautions you can take if you're concerned.

- I always place my slow cookers on top of my ceramic cooktop. This surface is designed to withstand high temperatures, after all. Just be sure never to accidentally have a hotplate turned on (I lost my first ever slow cooker to this happening when I melted its legs off!). If you don't have this option, placing the cooker on a glass-top trivet or heavy cutting board works in a similar way.
- Ensure flammable objects are not left touching or anywhere near the slow cooker.
- Move the slow cooker away from the wall and any curtains, etc.
- Do not use the tea towel method if you are out of the house.
- Always have a working smoke alarm and electrical safety switch in your home so that if you are home and the worst somehow happens, you and your family will be alerted to the danger and the electricity supply will shut off.

Is it okay to open the lid of my slow cooker to stir my dish or check on it?

Many of us have heard the tale that each time you open the lid of your slow cooker, it adds 30 minutes to the cooking time.

In practice, I have never personally found this to be true. If I am at home I am a habitual lid-lifter, often pausing to look at, stir, taste or even smell my dish throughout the day. And if anything, my dishes often cook much faster than I might expect.

However, slow cookers rely on the slow build-up of heat to cook food to perfection. Lifting the lid during cooking lets built-up heat escape and will lower the temperature in the slow cooker. Stirring the contents allows even more heat to escape from the lower layers of the food. Once the lid is replaced, it will take an amount of time for the food to heat back up to its previous temperature.

So the choice is up to you. Resist if you can, or don't. You will soon come to know your own slow cooker (or if you are like me and have several, you will get to know each of their little quirks and cooking times and temps).

Do I need to pre-brown, pre-cook or seal my meat before placing it in the slow cooker?

This is a debate that has no right or wrong answer. Some people are fierce advocates of browning meat prior to slow cooking it … while just as many are fiercely against doing so.

At the end of the day it comes down to your own personal choice.

But let's look at the reasons on both sides of the debate so you can decide what YOU want to do.

Reasons to brown

- Faster cooking time – meat that is pre-browned won't need as much cooking time.
- Lock in moisture – sealing the surface of the meat can seal in extra moisture.
- Increased flavour – those caramelised, brown yummy bits on the surface of your meat that come with browning have lots of flavour that would otherwise be missing from your finished dish. Browning with herbs or spices can also increase the richness of these flavours in your recipe.
- Appearance – sometimes despite no change in taste, browned meat benefits the presentation of the final dish. By contrast, meat juices released from unsealed meat can sometimes mix with sauces etc making it appear as if cream-based sauces have split, when they have not.
- Fat removal – browning meat before cooking and then discarding the liquids produced is a great way to eliminate some of the fat from your finished dish. This is especially true when browning mince or ground beef.
- Thickening – meat dredged in flour, then browned before slow cooking, will add to the thickness of the sauce in the final dish.

Reasons not to brown

- Convenience – this would have to be the number one reason. Many of us are drawn to slow cooking by the sheer convenience of pouring a collection of ingredients into the bowl, turning on the machine and walking away. This convenience is lessened when you have to add extra steps to pre-brown.

- Time factor – pre-browning meat tends to reduce the cooking time for the recipe. This works against many slow cookers who rely on the extended slow cooking period to make it work for them, for example when they work all day.
- Less mess – while many new slow cookers allow the option to sear in the same bowl as you slow cook, this is not possible with the traditional ceramic bowl slow cookers. Thus browning a dish means dirtying a frying pan. Let's face it, who likes extra dishes? Not me!
- No option – we see many of our members using slow cookers when they don't have access to stoves/ovens. In this instance they do not have the option to brown their meats but shouldn't think that means they can't slow cook a dish that asks for it.

In summary

It really is up to you.

Personally I very rarely brown – maybe 5 per cent of the time that I slow cook, and then it's almost only those recipes which call for thin strips of meat to be flour coated and browned prior to slow cooking.

Some days and with some recipes you will want to – others you'll want to just dump in your ingredients, set and forget. Neither way is right or wrong, but hopefully in these pages we have given you the information to decide what's right for you.

Can I slow cook a whole chicken?

You sure can! And many people will tell you that having tried slow cooking chickens whole they will never cook them any other way.

Here are some tips to keep in mind.

- You don't need to add any liquids to the slow cooker with your chicken. You will be really surprised by just how much liquid a whole chicken will release during cooking! And because a slow cooker is sealed, that liquid won't evaporate.

- Cook your chicken with the breast-side down. This keeps the breast meat sitting in the liquid that's produced during cooking so it won't dry out.
- If you are concerned there is too much liquid, or if you have a spice rub etc on your chicken that you don't want to get too immersed in liquid, you may choose to elevate the chicken above the bottom of your slow cooker by sitting it on some scrunched up aluminium foil balls, egg rings or even an inverted dish.
- When it comes to seasoning your chicken, your imagination is your only limit. Whatever spice, marinade or herbs you may use when you cook a chicken in the oven you can use just as well in your slow cooker.
- When your chicken is cooked it will be fall-apart tender! I like to get mine out in one piece by sliding two spatulas or large mixing spoons underneath both ends of the chicken and then quickly lifting it up and out onto a dish. An alternative method is to create a foil or baking-paper sling under your chicken prior to cooking. This can be used to grasp and lift the chicken out at the end of cooking. This can be a large sling design or two strips crossed over to form a basket of sorts. Whatever works for you!

Help! I accidently cooked the absorbent pad from under my raw meat…

That awful moment when you first spot it… you have made a lovely slow cooker meal and you are just giving it a little stir before you serve it, when it appears: the absorbent pad from under your raw meat has accidentally ended up in your slow cooker – and *gasp* – you've cooked it!

Oh no!

What now?

Is your meal ruined?

Do you have to throw it out?

This actually happens a lot. More than you'd realise. At least a few times a week we see a member of our Facebook group looking for advice on what to do when they realise they've done this. So our goal was to get to the bottom of it and what it means for you and your pot full of otherwise yummy slow cooked food.

What are they?

Absorbent meat pads or absorbent meat soakers are the little packages that often sit between your raw meat and your butcher's tray. The purpose of the pad is to catch and absorb the liquid that naturally drains from raw meat and would otherwise pool in your meat tray and potentially spill out on you when it was tilted. It also helps prevent meat from sitting in a pool of raw meat juice that could breed bacteria and reduce shelf life.

The fact they are often black to begin with or soaked red with juices means that it's easier than you may think to tip your raw meat into your slow cooker from the tray without realising you have tipped in the pad as well.

What are they made of?

The butchers that I spoke to explained that the pads are usually made from paper pulp, plant fibres or non-toxic silicone with a plastic outer layer. They explained that they are approved for use in contact with food that is intended for human consumption, which means they have to be food-safe and non-toxic. They are not digestible, which means that even if you ate one it would go right through your digestive tract.

But what about when they are cooked? Does that change things?

Do I need to throw my meal in the bin?

The general consensus seems to be – if the pad is broken or pierced in any way, sadly yes, you should throw your meal out.

However, if the pad is intact you may decide to still eat your meal if you are comfortable doing so. A manufacturer of these pads (www.thermasorb.com.au) advises that if they are not broken then your meal is okay to eat. The poisons information hotline people agree. They report getting a lot of calls regarding this issue and advise that if the packet is broken your meal should be discarded just to be safe. However, in their experience, if the packet is intact most people will have no ill effects. From their experience, at worst those with a sensitive stomach may experience mild nausea or an unpleasant taste, but this is rare and most of their callers experience no ill effects.

So the choice is ultimately yours.

Help! My cream has split

In our slow cooking community we often see members posting their concern over split cream in their slow cooked dishes.

What is splitting?
A lot of people will refer to dairy products that have split as being 'curdled'. If your dairy product curdles during storage that's a problem and you should throw it out; don't use it. However, if it separates during cooking, it's more likely to be split and that is really only a change of appearance and texture. It's still perfectly fine to eat.

Why does it occur?
Sauces made with dairy products can split for several reasons.

- Low fat content – dairy products with high fat content are less likely to split.
- High heat – exposing dairy products to high heat, eg close to boiling, increases the likelihood of splitting.
- High acidity – adding dairy products to recipes with elevated acidic content can also cause splitting.

How can I prevent it?
- Choose higher-fat versions of your dairy product rather than the low fat varieties.
- If possible add the dairy product at the end of your cooking time rather than the beginning. You can even take it off the heat before you add it.
- When adding cream early, try whisking a teaspoon or so of cornflour into the cream first before adding it to your dish.
- Choose 'cooking cream' or 'creme fraiche' or double cream – these are less likely to split.
- Allow dairy products to come to room temperature before adding them. This can also help.
- Adding cream to a water-based recipe can cause splitting. Stirring regularly helps to avoid this.

What do I do once it's happened?

- Remember … it's okay to eat. While a dish with split cream may not look perfect, it's certainly NOT a reason to throw it out!
- If the nature of the dish allows it, try giving the food a really good stir or whisk.
- Alternatively, try stirring through a little cornflour and water slurry.

Don't be discouraged! Next time just try the preventative measures. If all else fails, eat your meal with your eyes shut and you'll never know the difference *wink*.

Can I prepare a meal in advance and store it in the slow cooker bowl in my fridge overnight, then put it on the next morning?

Yes, you can if you wish. But it comes with risks!

Heating a cold bowl can lead to it cracking.

Also, the bowl and its contents will retain that cold for a long time and thus take even longer to reach safe temperatures once you begin cooking, placing you at increased risk of food poisoning.

A great way around this is to prepare the dish in advance but store it in the fridge in another large bowl, for example a mixing bowl. The food can then be poured into the slow cooker bowl in the morning. You still have all the convenience but without any of the risk.

Can I add pasta to my dish?

I often get asked about adding pasta to slow cooker recipes. Can you add raw pasta to your dish, or cooked pasta? Yes you can!

The fast option is to add cooked or almost cooked pasta shortly before your meal has finished cooking. Like any pasta, you don't want to overcook it, so if it's been pre-cooked then only leave it in there long enough to heat through with the rest of the recipe. Alternatively, cook the pasta separately and serve with your slow cooker dish at plating time.

But what if you want to add raw pasta to your recipe? That's an option too. But there are some factors that you'll need to keep in mind…

- When you add raw pasta to your recipe you need to have enough liquid to accommodate it. While cooking, the raw pasta will absorb a lot of liquid from your recipe. This is a great way to thicken your dish if that's what you want, but it can spell disaster if your dish is already fairly dry. So if you know you will be adding pasta, be sure you add enough extra liquid at the start (or with the pasta) to accommodate it – without watering down your flavours.
- As a general rule, add raw pasta about 45 minutes prior to serving.
- Different types of pasta may of course cook in different time frames based on size and thickness, so for the first time check it occasionally to know when it's done to your pasta preferences.

What is the best way to clean my slow cooker bowl?

It happens to all of us sometimes! We finish cooking our recipe only to find a baked-on ring of cooked or burnt residue inside our slow cooker or on the base. Or maybe the inner casing of your slow cooker has stains in it? Don't despair – we've got the solution!

Basics
- The sooner you get it off the better!
- Avoid harsh abrasive chemicals or cleaning scourers.
- Always unplug the unit from the power source before cleaning.

Cleaning inside the cooking bowl
Most slow cooker bowls can simply be washed by hand in the sink. Some are okay for washing in the dishwasher. Be sure to check your manual for what is suitable for your model as not all models are dishwasher safe.

However, if you find yourself with a baked-on ring around the bowl that's hard to remove, the easiest way to get rid of it is remove the food, add water to a level above the baked-on ring and leave the slow cooker turned to LOW for a couple of hours. The ring should clean away much more easily then.

Some suggest placing a dishwasher tablet or even a denture cleaning tablet in the slow cooker while the water is heating in it for up to two hours but it is advisable to check with your user manual whether this is safe for your model.

Ceramic bowls and lids will not withstand sudden temperature changes. Do not fill the bowl with cold water when it is hot as it will crack.

Some ceramic bowls have a porous base and should not be left standing in water for extended periods because they might absorb water. It's fine to fill inside the bowl with water and leave it for any amount of time, but avoid leaving the entire bowl standing IN water.

Cleaning inside the main casing of the slow cooker

The metal housing of the slow cooker and electrical lead should NOT be placed in water! Be sure to completely unplug your unit from the power source and allow it to cool before any cleaning.

Over time you will find some of your food will splash down into the main casing of your slow cooker – under the cooking bowl.

It is important to ALWAYS CHECK YOUR INSTRUCTION MANUAL FIRST as to how your manufacturer recommends you clean your slow cooker.

Normally, electrical cables inside the base unit are fully sealed, but you should still exercise extreme caution in cleaning this main base unit – and again, never place the unit itself in water. If you can see heating elements inside the base do not clean or add water in this area and instead contact the manufacturer for advice.

For those who wish to proceed with cleaning inside the main casing, here are some suggestions I have gathered from members of the Slow Cooker Central community.

- Simply wipe the spill off with a soft, damp cloth and a small amount of dish detergent, especially if the spill is fresh or new.
- Clean using a mix of baking soda and vinegar on a cloth or sponge.
- Use a chalk-based cleaning paste like Gumption, which you can find in your supermarket cleaning aisle.
- Use baking soda and lemon juice. Combine and allow to foam then apply with a soft pad, sponge or scourer.
- While a soft green scrubbing type pad scourer should be okay, please think carefully before using a stronger steel wool type scourer as you could scratch your inner casing or bowl. A gentle sponge or rubber based scrubbing tool is ideal.
- Some report using a thin coat of oven cleaner (a fume-free version if you can), left for an hour or so then wiped off. If doing this I would

recommend wiping over a few times with a damp cloth to minimise any smells next time you use the unit. Note: oven cleaners can be caustic and may even dissolve paint on the outside of your cooker, so use sparingly and cautiously.

Prevention is best

Rather than deal with the clean-up, try to prevent spills where you can!

- Spray your slow cooker bowl with some non-stick cooking spray before beginning.
- Line your slow cooker with baking paper for baked items or ones you think may stick.
- Use a slow-cooker liner bag or even an oven bag to slow-cook your dish.
- Follow the cooking time recommended in the recipe and avoid overcooking and burning.
- Do not overfill your slow cooker, which would increase the likelihood of spilling and staining in the casing area.

Should I pack my slow cooker away in summer?

As someone who slow cooks *all year* round, I've never been one to subscribe to the old school of thought that it's only a winter appliance. As a result, I'm often asked about what I slow cook in hot summer months. Here I'll give you some ideas…

I personally don't find one slow cooker on the go in my kitchen makes any difference whatsoever to the temperature in my house during a hot Queensland summer. But if you feel otherwise, try running your slow cooker in your garage, laundry or patio etc. It's certainly better than standing over a stove or oven in a hot kitchen, that's for sure!

Another option is to slow cook overnight or very early morning before the temperature starts to soar. Or slow cook a few meals at once so you don't have to cook again at all the next day :)

The most important determinate of summer slow cooking is the sides. Sure, you aren't likely to cook soups or hot curries or big hearty hot casseroles, but that leaves plenty of other options, and if you change what you serve on the side, you change the season of the dish! Ditch the hot vegetables, the rice and the mash or heavy pastas and serve your slow cooked meal with salads or on light wraps, as pizza toppings or even as nibble platters and with BBQ sides!

I find most of our egg based recipes to be light and summery. Who doesn't love a quiche, an omelette or a frittata with a lovely side salad on a hot day! Or go to our chicken chapter for recipes like wings, chicken drumsticks or even slow cooked whole chickens which, again, go great with a salad or with wraps or BBQ-style sides. Or perhaps something from our seafood chapter with chips and salad – that sounds summery!

Another great option is cold cuts of roast meat! Roast pork, beef or lamb … all great served cold on a steamy hot day with a nice fresh salad. And don't forget ribs! Always delish with a light side on a hot day!

And who can go past a simple pulled meat! So easy to serve on a bread roll with salad or slaw for an easy, light summer feed,

Of course you may just rather skip cooking the main meals and slow cook other things like desserts, cakes, fudges, snacks or side dishes too.

Whatever you decide, we have it for you here in these pages to get you through those hot steamy days of summer slow cooking.

Are there any 'diet' recipes for slow cookers?

Almost every recipe can be adapted for weight loss or to make it healthier (with some obvious dessert-type exceptions).

Ways to adapt recipes to make them more waist-friendly include:

- Choose lean. Choose leaner cuts of meat than the recipe specifies. For example, go with low-fat mince, low-fat sausages or skinless chicken.
- Brown and bin. Brown meats before you slow cook them. This gives you an opportunity to drain and discard the fat rather than include it in your slow cooking recipe. Some people even like to boil their mince before cooking to remove fat.
- Trim the fat. Remove the fat before cooking, or remove fat or skin from the completed dish before serving.
- Bulk up. Add extra vegetables to your meal. If the dish you are cooking has few or no vegetables why not add some during cooking? Or when it comes to plating up your meal, load your plate with steamed or stir-fried veg to fill you up.
- Slash the salt. Choose low-sodium options for your ingredients. Even if the recipe doesn't specify it, I often change things like soy sauce or stocks to low-sodium options to cut the salt from the overall recipe.

- Choose low fat. In the same way that you can substitute low-salt ingredients, do the same with low-fat ones. Opt for low-fat yoghurts, milks and cheese, for example – pretty much anything that has a low-fat option.
- Selecting sides. What can make or break a meal when it comes to your waistline is sides. Choose wisely and your scales will thank you. Opt for healthier options like vegetables, salads and brown rice and the impact of the main meal is less.
- Portion power. Healthy eating is largely about moderation. You can enjoy that meal you really want, without having to totally overdo it. It's better to consume small portions of the foods that you crave rather than trying to resist them totally and ending up blowing out on a binge. Match the portion sizes of the various food groups on your plate with recommendations for a balanced and healthy diet.
- Love your leftovers. Why not cook extra when you do your next slow cooker meal? Then you can portion and store leftovers into healthy-sized meals all ready to take to work or to grab when the next attack of munchies strikes. It makes you less likely to make poor choices on impulse or opt for unhealthy take-away food.
- More of the same. As with all healthy eating plans, don't forget the basics. Drink plenty of water, eat mindfully, pack heaps of variety into your meal plans, choose fresh food when you can and move more!

Is it toxic to slow cook raw red kidney beans?

Yes, it is! But only raw beans. This does *not* include the canned varieties that are already cooked. A good explanation can be found at www. choosingvoluntarysimplicity.com:

'Raw kidney beans contain especially large amounts of [phytohaemag-glutinin], and amazingly, eating just four or five raw or improperly cooked kidney beans can make a person extremely ill. Ingesting larger amounts can actually cause death. Other beans, including white kidney beans, broad beans and lima beans, contain the same toxin in smaller but still dangerous amounts.'

If you'd like to read further on this issue, these websites would be good starting points:

- www.choosingvoluntarysimplicity.com/crockpots-slow-cooking-dried-beans-phytohaemagglutinin/
- www.medic8.com/healthguide/food-poisoning/red-kidney-bean-toxins.html

Slow cooking cakes

Cooking cakes in slow cookers is out of the norm for a lot of traditionalist slow cooker users, so we wanted to include some advice on what can and can't be used in cake making in your slow cooker, and also to provide some general tips for getting the most out of your slow cooker cake making.

First and foremost, as detailed on page 7, the 'tea towel trick' is very important to prevent condensation dripping on your cakes when cooking them in the slow cooker.

Slow cookers can be used to cook packet (box) cake mixes as well as your own favourite from-scratch recipe.

But what do you cook the actual cake in?

There are three options.

1. Line your slow cooker inner bowl and cook your cake directly in it.

When doing this I find lining the bowl with non-stick baking paper not only prevents sticking but also gives you something to hold onto so you can lift the cake out at the end of the cooking time.

2. Cook your cake in a metal cake tin.

If you are concerned about using a metal cake tin dry in your slow cooker (ceramic bowls in particular are unsuitable for dry cooking) simply fill the bottom of the slow cooker bowl with 2–3 cm (1 in) of water first, then sit your cake tin gently in this water.

You can also elevate the cake tin off the bottom of the slow cooker to allow heat to circulate evenly around your cake. This can be achieved by resting the cake tin on a metal trivet, on metal egg rings or even on scrunched up balls of aluminium foil.

3. Cook your cake in a silicone cake tin.

Silicone cake tins (full size and cupcake size) are also safe to use in your slow cooker and will not melt. After all, they are intended for the high heat of conventional ovens.

When using non-ceramic slow cooker bowls I personally sit my silicone cake tins/cups directly onto the bottom of the slow cooker, without water, with no concerns. But if you prefer, you can elevate your tin using the methods described above. When using a ceramic cooker bowl I again add water first.

As with all non-traditional slow cooking, be sure to check your manual first and only do what you are comfortable doing.

Slow cooker fudge FAQs

Our members LOVE cooking fudge! We have hundreds of different varieties on the website, so you can browse for fudge online or use one of the recipes in this book. I've compiled some commonly asked questions about fudge to help you along the way.

What type of chocolate can I use?

Any type. Change the flavour of the chocolate to change the taste of the fudge. Milk chocolate, white chocolate, hazelnut chocolate, cookies and cream chocolate ... the options are unlimited. Some members use cooking chocolate, but others say the taste is not the same, so use your judgement. (Cooking chocolate does tend to melt at higher temperatures, so regular chocolate is ideal for the lower temp of the slow cooker.) If you are using chocolate that has a liquid-type filling, eg Caramello, you will need to increase the chocolate amount to account for this.

Can I add chocolate and lollies to my fudge

Yes. You can mix or top your fudge with anything you like. Make the base fudge, stir through whatever you like to add, then pour it into the lined tin to set. For example, you could add chopped nuts, biscuits, Mars bars, lollies (candies) ... whatever you like. Or pour your fudge into your tray to set then decorate the surface with these types of toppings. Again the options are endless.

How do I actually cook it? Do I need to stir it?

Break up the chocolate and place it in your slow cooker. Pour over condensed milk and add the butter and vanilla. LEAVE THE LID OFF your slow cooker and turn it on low and walk away. Every 10–15 minutes just pass by and give it a stir. It's that easy. As you near the end of the cooking time you may need to keep a closer eye on it but really it's just the odd stir along the way and there is nothing else to do.

Can I use any spoon to stir?

It's ideal to use a metal or silicone spoon when stirring your fudge. A wooden spoon can absorb some of the liquid from your fudge so it's best to avoid these. (Not to mention the fact that a metal spoon is a little nicer to lick clean!)

My fudge has seized – how can I fix it?

If things don't go to plan, your fudge might seize, which means it turns hard and weird instead of glossy. This problem can result from water getting into the fudge – remember, lids off for fudge to avoid condensation drips. Using a wooden spoon can do the same – remember, use a metal, plastic or silicone spoon for stirring fudge. There are a few approaches our members use to rescue seized fudge. Try stirring the living daylights out of it to bring it back to glossy. Others add a little splash of milk or condensed milk or even a bit more chocolate then stir like the clappers to bring it all back together. All is not lost. This is fixable – stir stir stir!

How do I know when it's done?

Everyone's slow cooker takes a different amount of time to cook. Simply melting the chocolate is not enough. After some time, you'll notice a very slight 'crust' on the surface as you stir, and the mixture will come away from the edges of the bowl slightly. This is the best sign that it's done. Some larger (hotter) machines may achieve this in half an hour. My 1.5 litre cooker that I use for fudge takes more like 90 minutes to achieve this. You will get to know yours.

What do I do with it once it's cooked?

Stir through any extras you want to add, then pour your fudge into a slice tray (I use one approximately 20cm x 20cm) lined with baking paper. You can use silicone moulds instead if you choose. Smooth the surface down to flat and add any decorations you like. If nothing is being added then simply place your tray in the fridge until set – approximately four hours should do it. Then use the baking paper to lift out your fudge from the tray. Remove the paper and cut the fudge quickly. Dipping your knife into hot water first can help cut cleanly.

How should I store my fudge?

Store your fudge in a sealed container in the fridge (make it a non-transparent container if you want to keep it from being rapidly gobbled up by the fudge fanatics in your home *wink*). The fudge will keep up to four weeks in a fridge. It can also be frozen for up to three months.

My fudge didn't set. What did I do wrong?

Please review the above tips. One of them will most likely reveal the reason your fudge did not set. You could also try returning your fudge to the slow cooker to reheat, adding more chocolate, then cooking it for longer. Not using enough chocolate is the number one cause of fudge not setting.

Pantry staples

One of the best ways to ease into trying new recipes is to have a supply of staple items in your pantry – on hand and at the ready for your next kitchen session. Build up your collection and all future recipes will be even friendlier on your budget.

Useful staples include:

- Baking powder
- Balsamic vinegar
- Canned or dried fruits
- Canned or dried vegetables
- Canned soups: condensed cream soups in various flavours (especially cream of mushroom and cream of chicken)
- Coconut cream and milk
- Cornflour
- Couscous
- Curry powder
- Dry packet soups such as French onion and chicken noodle
- Flour: plain (all-purpose) and self-raising
- Garlic: fresh or minced in jar
- Ginger: fresh or minced in jar
- Gravy powder/granules
- Herbs and spices: fresh in your garden, frozen in tubes or dried in jars and packets – as many as you can gather!
- Honey
- Lentils
- Mustard powder
- Parmesan: fresh or dried
- Pasta
- Pepper
- Powdered milk or UHT milk
- Rice
- Salt
- Sauces: sweet chilli, BBQ, tomato, worcestershire, soy, mint, oyster, hoisin
- Stock: powder, cubes or long life liquid (especially beef, chicken and vegetable)
- Sugar: brown and white
- Sweetened condensed milk
- Tinned tomatoes
- Tinned tuna
- Tomato paste
- Vinegar
- Wine: red and white
- Yeast

This is by no means an exhaustive list but it's a great start!

Goodbye, oven. Hello slow cooker! Converting oven and stovetop recipes for your slow cooker

Now you're hooked on slow cooking, I bet you'll find there are heaps of your family's favourite recipes that you have always cooked in the oven or on the stovetop that you want to convert for a slow cooker. And, for almost all of them, there is no reason you can't!

Here are some simple pointers:

- Reduce the amount of liquid. The condensation that forms in your slow cooker when in use means that recipes cooked in slow cookers need much less liquid then their traditional stovetop or oven counterparts. As a general rule try reducing the total liquid by approximately one quarter.
- Use cheaper cuts of meat. Remember that almost any cut of meat – even the cheapest and toughest – is sure to be tender after slow cooking. So feel free to replace more expensive cuts of meat with a cheaper option.
- Adjust the amounts of herbs and spices. Many people recommend reducing them by one half when converting a regular recipe for a slow cooker.
- Adjust the time. See the chart below to convert your stove and oven times to slow cooker times.
- Arrange the ingredients. When filling your slow cooker, put the root vegetables around the bottom and sides of your slow cooker, then place your meat on top.
- Take notes and experiment. It may take some trial and error to tweak your old favourites but it'll be worth it. Adjust liquids as you go (adding or removing) and keep an eye on cooking times. Take notes as you try new things so you'll always know just what worked the best for you. Soon you'll have a recipe you can use anywhere!

Stovetop & Oven Cooking Times	Slow Cooking on LOW Cooking Times	Slow Cooking on HIGH Cooking Times
15–30 mins	4–6 hours	1½–2½ hours
45 mins–1 hour	6½–8 hours	3–4 hours
1½–2½ hours	9–12 hours	4½–6 hours
3–5 hours	12½–18 hours	5–7 hours

SOUP

⊨— Homemade Chicken Stock —●

Making stock in a slow cooker couldn't be easier – I'll never buy ready-made chicken stock again. The flavours are so much richer and the smell while it's cooking is lovely.

Makes 1.9 litres (4 pints) • Preparation 5 mins • Cook 20 hours • Cooker capacity 6 litres

1.5 kg (3 lb 5 oz) whole chicken
2 onions, halved
2 carrots, coarsely chopped
2 celery stalks, coarsely chopped
1 teaspoon whole black peppercorns
½ garlic bulb, halved horizontally
1 leek, coarsely chopped
3 thyme sprigs
3 rosemary sprigs
4 fresh or dried bay leaves

1. Combine all the ingredients in the slow cooker. Add water to about 2½ cm (1 inch) from the top of the slow cooker bowl. Cover and cook on low for up to 20 hours to develop the full depth of flavour.

2. Remove and discard the solids using a slotted spoon. Strain the liquid through a fine sieve into a large bowl. If you don't have a sieve, you could use a leg cut from a new, clean pair of pantyhose – stretch it over a large bowl to make a sieve.

3. Refrigerate the stock overnight to chill thoroughly.

4. Carefully remove the layer of solidified fat from the top of the stock.

5. Refrigerate and use within 3–4 days or freeze and use within 3 months.

Minestrone Soup

This recipe makes a large, filling, fresh soup that's perfect served with a buttered crusty bread roll to dunk in your bowl. Packed with pasta and vegetables, it's a hearty meal great for a large crowd.

Serves 8–10 • Preparation 20 mins • Cook 9–10 hours • Cooker capacity 6 litres

4 cups vegetable stock
2 x 400 g (14 oz) cans diced Italian tomatoes
400 g (14 oz) can cannellini beans, drained and rinsed
3 potatoes, skin on, diced into 1cm cubes
4–6 celery stalks, sliced
3 carrots, diced into 1cm cubes
2 large brown onions, diced
1 large handful green beans, coarsely chopped
⅓ cup tomato paste
2 tablespoons fresh basil, thinly sliced
1 tablespoon minced garlic
2 teaspoons dried oregano
2 teaspoons dried thyme
1 teaspoon cracked black pepper
½ teaspoon salt
1 large zucchini, diced into 1cm cubes
100 g (3½ oz) baby spinach leaves
½ cup macaroni
Crusty bread rolls, to serve

1. Combine all the ingredients except the zucchini, spinach and pasta in the slow cooker. Cover and cook on low for 8–9 hours.

2. Add the zucchini, spinach and pasta and cook for another hour.

3. Serve with crusty bread rolls for a vegetarian feast of goodness.

Chinese Chicken Noodle and Sweet Corn Soup

A classic chicken and corn soup with a Chinese twist, perfect as an entrée or a main on its own.

Serves 4 • Preparation 15 mins • Cook 5 hours 10 mins • Cooker capacity 5 litres

4 cups chicken stock
4 skinless chicken thigh fillets
420g (15 oz) can corn kernels
420g (15 oz) can creamed corn
2 tablespoons soy sauce
1 tablespoon minced ginger
1 tablespoon minced garlic
2 teaspoons sesame oil
2 eggs, whisked
72 g (2½ oz) packet two-minute noodles (no seasoning)
1 cup spring onions (scallions), thinly sliced, plus extra to garnish

1. Combine all the ingredients except the egg, noodles and spring onion in the slow cooker. Cover and cook on low for 5 hours.
2. Remove chicken, shred and return to slow cooker.
3. Whisk soup, then pour in egg, whisking continuously to create ribbons of egg.
4. Stir in noodles and spring onion and cook for another 10 minutes.
5. Serve garnished with extra spring onion.

Zesty Tomato Soup

This fresh, made-from-scratch tomato soup is a warming entrée or main course on a cold winter's night. You can make it creamy or non-creamy, vegetarian or non-vegetarian.

Serves 4 • Preparation 15 mins • Cook 5 hours • Cooker capacity 3 litres

2 x 400 g (14 oz) cans diced tomatoes
2 cups chicken stock (see note)
1 onion, finely diced
1 celery stalk, finely diced
3 tablespoons fresh basil, thinly sliced, or 1 tablespoon dried basil, plus extra fresh basil leaves to garnish
2 tablespoons brown sugar
2 garlic cloves, minced
1 teaspoon cracked black pepper
200 ml (7 fl oz) cooking cream (optional; see note)

1. Combine all the ingredients except the cream and extra basil in the slow cooker. Cover and cook on high for 5 hours.

2. Stir in the cream (see note), then blend with a stick blender until smooth.

3. Divide between bowls and garnish with extra basil.

NOTES: Replace the chicken stock with vegetable stock if you want to create a vegetarian version.

If you prefer a non-creamy soup, omit the cream.

Curried Carrot Soup

I wasn't expecting to like this recipe as much as I did. It was so good that I ended up eating the leftovers the next day for lunch when everyone else was at school and work, so that I didn't have to share it. It makes a thick soup that's great as a vegetarian entrée.

Serves 4 • Preparation 20 mins • Cook 5 hours • Cooker capacity 5 litres

700 g (1 lb 9 oz) carrots (about 5 large), coarsely chopped
2 cups vegetable stock
300 g (10½ oz) potatoes (about 2), coarsely chopped
1 large onion, diced
1 teaspoon curry powder, or to taste
1 teaspoon salt
1 teaspoon cracked black pepper

1. Combine all the ingredients in the slow cooker. Cover and cook on high for 5 hours or until the vegetables are lovely and tender.

2. Blend with a stick blender until smooth, then serve.

Easy Pea and Ham Soup

Pea and ham soup is a classic slow-cooker meal but I like to make things even easier by using meat that's already been taken off the bone so there's no need to do it at the end of cooking. If your butcher doesn't sell the ready cut chunks, use several ham hocks. Once cooked, discard the fat, cut the meat into chunks and return it to the soup.

Serves 8 • Preparation 10 mins • Cook 6–8 hours • Cooker capacity 6 litres

500 g–1 kg (1 lb 2 oz–2 lb 4 oz) green split peas (depending on how thick you like your soup), rinsed and drained
2 onions, coarsely chopped
750 g (1 lb 10½ oz) diced bacon chunks off the bone (not regular bacon)
6 cups water
Crusty bread rolls, to serve

1. Put the split peas, onion and bacon chunks in the slow cooker. Add water to fill to 5 cm (2 inches) below the top of the slow cooker. Cover and cook for 6–8 hours on low, until the soup has thickened nicely and the split peas have all broken down.

2. Serve in big bowls with crusty bread rolls on the side.

Super Easy Chicken Soup

You can throw this together in a flash and know that a beautiful chicken soup will await you at day's end. Winner, winner, chicken dinner! Very good for the soul.

Serves 6–8 • Preparation 10 mins • Cook 8 hours• Cooker capacity 6 litres

1–2 kg (2 lb 4 oz–4 lb 8 oz) chicken wings and/or drumsticks
500 g (1 lb 2 oz) frozen diced vegetables
2 onions, diced
40 g (1½ oz) dry chicken noodle soup mix
2–3 tablespoons chicken stock powder
Crusty bread rolls, to serve

1. Put all the ingredients in the slow cooker. Fill with water to about 5 cm (2 inches) below the top of the inner bowl. Cover and cook for 8 hours on low.

2. Take the chicken out, remove the bones, return the chicken meat to the soup and stir.

3. Serve with crusty bread rolls.

Classic Creamy Pumpkin Soup

This was my first ever attempt at cooking a pumpkin soup, let alone a slow-cooker version. I was thrilled to receive a rousing 'hoorah' from seasoned pumpkin soup lovers. The toasted pumpkin seeds on top are optional. Serve with crusty bread rolls and a dollop of cream stirred through.

Serves 12 • Preparation 20 mins • Cook 6 hours • Cooker capacity 6 litres

1 large jarrahdale or butternut pumpkin (squash), peeled and chopped
1 large potato, chopped
2 carrots, chopped
2 onions, chopped
2 garlic cloves, minced
3 cups chicken stock

GARNISH
½ teaspoon olive oil
2 tablespoons dried pumpkin seeds
Cream or sour cream
Garlic chives

1. Put all the ingredients for the soup in the slow cooker. Cover and cook on low for 6 hours.

2. Blend with a stick blender until smooth.

3. Heat the olive oil in a small frying pan over medium heat. Add the pumpkin seeds and stir constantly for 3–5 minutes, or until golden.

4. Serve the pumpkin soup with a dollop of cream or sour cream, scattered with chives and toasted pumpkin seeds.

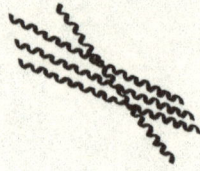

PASTA

Meatlover's Spaghetti and Meatballs

I blame my children for this recipe (ha ha). They love spaghetti bolognaise and they love meatballs, but they find tomato sauces less exciting. So we decided to cook the meatballs in a meaty sauce rather than a plain tomato one. I succeeded in my mission to please: it was cleaned plates all round and requests for seconds! Why not try it for your little ones too.

Serves 5 • Preparation 15 mins • Cook 7 hours • Cooker capacity 5 litres

700 g (1 lb 8½ oz) bottle tomato passata (puréed tomato)
500 g (1 lb 2 oz) minced (ground) pork
1 large brown onion, diced
1 tablespoon minced garlic
1 tablespoon dried Italian herbs
1 tablespoon tomato paste (concentrated purée)
20 premade raw beef meatballs
Spaghetti (cooked), to serve
Grated cheese, to serve

1. Combine all the ingredients except the meatballs in the slow cooker. Season with salt and pepper. Cover and cook on low for 4 hours.

2. Add the meatballs gently to the sauce and cook for another 3 hours. To ensure the meatballs remain intact, do not stir until just before serving.

3. Serve on spaghetti with a topping of your favourite grated cheese.

Tomato and Pesto Chicken Pasta

This sauce is fantastic on whatever pasta you love. The burst of basil complements the fresh tomatoes perfectly.

Serves 5 • Preparation 15 mins • Cook 4–5 hours • Cooker capacity 3 litres

750 g (1 lb 10½ oz) chicken thigh fillets
400 g (14 oz) can diced tomatoes
190 g (6½ oz) jar basil pesto
1 tablespoon minced garlic
125 g (4½ oz) cherry tomatoes, halved
Penne, to serve
Grated parmesan cheese, to serve
Fresh basil leaves, to serve

1. Combine the chicken, diced tomatoes, pesto and garlic in the slow cooker. Cover and cook on low for 4–5 hours, until the chicken is very tender.

2. Remove the chicken, shred it and return it to the slow cooker. Stir in the cherry tomatoes. Let the sauce continue to cook while you boil the penne separately.

3. Serve the sauce on the penne, garnished with parmesan and basil.

Homemade Tomato Pasta Sauce

Confession: I always used to buy pasta sauce in jars. In my mind, it was too time-consuming or expensive to make my own. How wrong I was! It's as easy as throwing everything into your slow cooker and just walking away. Then you can store it for future use, or use it right away – add your bolognaise ingredients to the cooker and dinner is done. Fresh tastes best, and it takes minimal fuss with this great from-scratch recipe.

Serves 6 • Preparation 15 mins • Cook 6 hours • Cooker capacity 6 litres

3 x 400 g (14 oz) cans diced tomatoes (see note)
1 large brown onion (pepper), diced
½ green capsicum (pepper), diced
⅓ cup (firmly packed) fresh basil, chopped
2 tablespoons tomato paste (concentrated purée)
1 tablespoon sugar
1 tablespoon Worcestershire sauce
4 garlic cloves, minced, or 1 heaped tablespoon minced garlic
2 teaspoons dried oregano
1 teaspoon cracked black pepper
½ teaspoon salt

1. Combine all the ingredients in the slow cooker. Cover and cook on low for 6 hours.

2. Use immediately, or cool and freeze. The sauce will keep, frozen, for 4 months.

NOTES: If you'd rather use fresh tomatoes, you'll need 1.2 kg (2 lb 10 oz) tomatoes. Cut a cross into the skin on the base of each tomato. Add to a large pot of boiling water and boil for 1 minute. Remove using a slotted spoon and place straight into a bowl of cold water. Remove the skin – it will peel off easily. Chop, crush or blend the tomatoes, then proceed as for canned tomatoes.

To make spaghetti bolognaise sauce, add 1 kg (2 lb 3 oz) minced (ground) beef and some chopped mushrooms to the hot sauce at the end of the cooking time, then cook for another 2–3 hours. Alternatively, use sauce from the freezer. Thaw it, add the mince and mushrooms, and cook for 4 hours on low.

Creamy, Cheesy Chicken and Tomato Pasta Bake

This is a great one-dish meal the whole family will love. The creamy, cheesy sauce is cooked right along with the chicken and pasta, so all you have to do is serve and enjoy.

Serves 5 • Preparation 20 mins • Cook 4¾ hours • Cooker capacity 6 litres

1 kg (2 lb 3 oz) chicken fillets (breast or thigh), diced
600 ml (20 fl oz) cooking cream
1 red onion, diced
190 g (6½ oz) jar tomato or sundried tomato pesto
2 garlic cloves, minced, or 1 tablespoon minced garlic
1–2 teaspoons cracked black pepper, to taste
1 cup small pasta shells
½ cup spring onions (scallions), thinly sliced
1 cup grated tasty cheese (see note)

1. Place the chicken in the slow cooker. Combine the cream, onion, pesto, garlic and pepper in a small bowl. Pour the mixture over chicken. Cover and cook on low for 3½–4 hours, until chicken is tender.

2. Stir in pasta and spring onion and cook for another 30 minutes. (Large pasta shells might need 45 minutes.)

3. Stir in cheese and cook for another 15 minutes or until cheese is melted.

4. Serve with steamed greens or on its own.

NOTE: I use light cheese, but full fat is fine too.

Cheesy Chicken and Chorizo Ravioli

Don't have the time or inclination to make your own ravioli? You don't need to! Choose whichever kind of ready-made ravioli you like best to form the base of this dish, and with a few extra steps you have a delicious pasta dish served with a chicken mince and chorizo sauce. You could swap the chicken mince for lean beef mince, which is more budget-friendly.

Serves 6 • Preparation 15 mins • Cook 4½ hours • Cooker capacity 5 litres

1 tablespoon olive oil
500 g (1 lb 2 oz) minced (ground) chicken
250 g (9 oz) chorizo sausage, diced
785 g (1 lb 11½ oz) bottle pasta sauce (I used tomato, onion and roasted garlic)
400 g (14 oz) can diced tomatoes
625 g (1 lb 6 oz) packet fresh ravioli or tortellini (I used roast chicken and garlic)
200 g (7 oz) grated mozzarella cheese
Garden salad and crusty garlic bread, to serve

1. Heat the oil in a searing slow cooker (or frying pan on the stovetop over medium-high heat) and cook the chicken mince and chorizo, breaking up lumps with a wooden spoon, until browned.

2. Combine the mince, chorizo, pasta sauce and tomatoes in the slow cooker.

3. Cover and cook on low for 4 hours.

4. Add the ravioli and stir to combine. Cook for 15 minutes, then sprinkle with cheese and cook for a further 15 minutes.

5. Serve with garden salad and crusty garlic bread.

One Pot Chicken Alfredo Pasta

Use leftover cooked chicken in this recipe, or grab a barbecue chicken on your way home. This is easy and tasty, and kids love to help make it.

Serves 4 • Preparation 20 mins • Cook 3¾ hours • Cooker capacity 6 litres

800 ml (27 fl oz) cooking cream
375 g (13 oz) block cream cheese, cubed
90 g (3 oz) butter, cubed
½ cup grated parmesan cheese
½ teaspoon garlic powder
½ teaspoon onion powder
Shredded cooked chicken, to taste (I used 2 breasts and some meat from the
    back of the whole chicken)
150 g (5½ oz) penne
½ cup grated parmesan cheese, extra

1. Combine the cream, cream cheese, butter, parmesan, garlic powder and onion powder in the slow cooker. Season with salt and pepper.

2. Cover and cook on low for 2 hours 45 minutes, stirring occasionally to break down the cream cheese.

3. Stir in the chicken and pasta. Cover and cook for 1 hour or until the pasta is cooked to your liking (the time may vary in different slow cookers). Keep an eye on it to make sure it doesn't dry out – add additional cream if needed.

4. Stir in the extra parmesan and serve.

NOTE: This makes a thick, creamy pasta. If you like a runnier, saucier Alfredo, then par-boil the pasta before adding it to the sauce. Cook for only 15 minutes or until the chicken is heated through and the pasta is tender. Semi-cooked or cooked pasta won't absorb as much of the sauce as raw pasta does. The cooking cream is important as it resists splitting like normal cream.

Spaghetti Bolognese

This bolognese sauce is just like my mum used to make. It's very saucy, and has the great tomato taste you want. There's no need to pre-brown the mince, and the sauce copes well with the 'keep warm' setting on the slow cooker. I like to use lean mince and skim any fat that rises to the top before serving.

Serves 6–8 • Preparation 15 mins • Cook 6 hours • Cooker capacity 5 litres

500 g (1 lb 2 oz) premium minced (ground) beef
500 g (1 lb 2 oz) tomato-based spaghetti sauce
200 g (7 oz) can condensed tomato soup
1 onion, finely diced
8 mushroom cups, coarsely chopped
1 large carrot, grated
3 tablespoons barbecue sauce
2 tablespoons Worcestershire sauce
2–3 garlic cloves, finely chopped
1 teaspoon dried Italian mixed herbs
Spaghetti and grated parmesan cheese, to serve

1. Combine all the ingredients in the slow cooker. Cover and cook on low for 6 hours.

2. Serve with spaghetti and grated parmesan cheese.

Cheesy One Pot Sausage and Veggie Pasta

A complete child-friendly meal served right from the slow cooker, this is sausages, pasta and vegetables with a cheesy twist. Kids of all ages will love this, and toddlers can perfect their self-feeding with this easy meal.

Serves 6 • Preparation 15 mins • Cook 5 hours 10 mins • Cooker capacity 6 litres

500 g (1 lb 2 oz) diced mixed vegetables (I used a bag of frozen veggies)
16 pork chipolata sausages, halved (or 8 regular pork sausages cut into quarters)
100 g (3½ oz) diced bacon
400 g (14 oz) can diced tomatoes
½ cup barbecue sauce
1 cup macaroni
1 cup grated tasty cheese
Parmesan cheese, optional, to serve

1. Place the vegetables into the slow cooker. Add the sausages and bacon. Combine the tomatoes, barbecue sauce and ½ cup water and pour over.

2. Cover and cook on low for 4½ hours.

3. Add another 1 cup hot water and the pasta. Cover and cook on low for a further 40 minutes or until the pasta is cooked to your liking. Keep an eye on it during this stage, as it may need extra water. Just add ½ cup at a time if you think it's needed.

4. Stir in the tasty cheese then serve, topped with a sprinkle of grated parmesan cheese if you like.

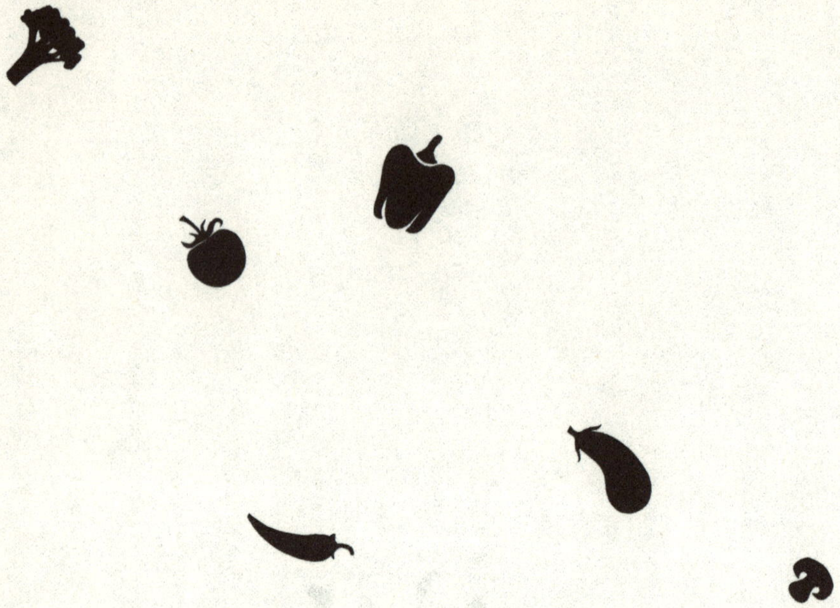

VEGETABLES

▄━ Loaded Cauliflower Bake ━●

This tasty side dish – cauliflower and bacon in a creamy sauce, topped with melted cheese – takes the humble cauliflower to the next level. It's great as part of a summer barbecue, a roast dinner with all the trimmings, or anything in between.

Serves 4 as a side dish • Preparation 10 mins • Cook 1¾–2 hours • Cooker capacity 3.5 litres

500 g (1 lb 2 oz) cauliflower, cut into pieces
100 g (3½ oz) diced bacon
300 ml (10 fl oz) cooking cream
½ teaspoon garlic powder
½ teaspoon cracked black pepper
2 teaspoons dried chives
1 cup grated tasty cheese

1. Arrange the cauliflower in the slow cooker and sprinkle with bacon.

2. Combine the cream, garlic powder and pepper and pour the mixture over the cauliflower.

3. Sprinkle with chives and top with grated cheese.

4. Cover, putting a tea towel (dish towel) under the lid, and cook on high for 1¾–2 hours, until the cauliflower is tender.

Mint Peas

As a child, I loved mint peas. We had them out of a tin back then, but as an adult I wanted to make my own. These have a mild hint of mint, nothing too overpowering, and go great as a side dish.

Serves 4 as a side dish • Preparation 5 mins • Cook 2 hours • Cooker capacity 1.5 litres

> 200 g (7 oz) frozen baby peas
> 1 cup vegetable stock
> 5 g packet lightly dried mint, or 1 tablespoon dried mint

1. Combine all the ingredients in the slow cooker. Cover and cook on low for 2 hours. Drain and serve.

NOTE: If you love mint, by all means increase the amount you use for more flavour.

Carrot and Parsnip Purée

A good friend of mine, Karen, grew up with her mum, Judi, making this dish, which features an old-school combination of vegetables. I'd never eaten parsnip before, but Karen convinced me it was really good, and she was right. This is so simple yet so tasty.

Serves 4 • Preparation 10 mins • Cook 2 hours • Cooker capacity 1.5 litres

300 g (10½ oz) carrots, chopped
200 g (7 oz) parsnips, chopped
1 tablespoon butter
¼ teaspoon ground nutmeg

1. Combine the carrot and parsnip in the slow cooker with 1 cup warm water. Cover and cook on high for 2 hours.

2. Drain well. Add butter and nutmeg, season with salt and pepper, and blend with a stick blender until smooth, or use a potato masher. Serve as a side dish.

Whole Cauliflower with Moroccan Butter Seasoning

When I was a dinner guest at a friend's house, I noticed the difficulties of cooking a whole cauliflower in a conventional oven: the edges tend to burn, and the centre tends to remain raw. Naturally, I thought how much better it would work in a slow cooker, and I decided to test the theory! After experimenting with some different flavours, I settled on this Moroccan butter seasoning, and I was amazed at how good a whole cauliflower could taste. It looks wonderful on a serving plate. To serve, cut it into wedges.

Serves 6-8 • Preparation 15 mins • Cook 5 hours • Cooker capacity 3.5 litres

1 whole cauliflower
50 g (1¾ oz) butter, melted
1½ teaspoons Moroccan spice mix
½ teaspoon garlic powder

1. Remove the leaves from the cauliflower, being careful to keep the cauliflower intact. Trim the stalk area to make a flat base. Place the whole cauliflower into the slow cooker, stalk side down.

2. Pierce the cauliflower to the centre with a large wooden or metal skewer in 10–15 places to help the flavour of the seasoning to penetrate.

3. Combine the melted butter, spice mix and garlic powder, then brush the mixture over the cauliflower using a pastry brush.

4. Cover and cook on low for 5 hours, basting the cauliflower with the cooking liquid a few times during cooking for a rich colour and flavour.

5. Remove carefully from the slow cooker and serve cut in wedges or slices.

Hasselback Sweet Potatoes

As a lover of sweet potatoes, I thought of slow-cooking them in the same hasselback style as regular potatoes. These are great with barbecue steak and salad.

Serves 4 • Preparation 20 mins • Cook 1½ hours • Cooker capacity 6 litres

2 large sweet potatoes, halved lengthways
2 tablespoons butter, melted
1 tablespoon honey
½ teaspoon ground cinnamon

1. Line the base of the slow cooker with baking paper.

2. Place a piece of sweet potato cut-side down on a chopping board. Make cuts along the potato at 5mm intervals, about two-thirds of the way through the sweet potato. Do not cut right through to the chopping board. Repeat with remaining sweet potato halves.

3. Arrange in the slow cooker, flat side down.

4. Combine the melted butter, honey and cinnamon, then brush the mixture over the sweet potatoes using a pastry brush.

5. Cover, putting a tea towel (dish towel) under the lid, and cook on high for 1½ hours or until tender.

6. Lift out carefully with an egg flip so as not to break the slices apart. Serve.

Coconut Curry Vegetables

A great vegetable side dish, or even a main course for our vegetarian fans. This is mild enough for the whole family to enjoy, but if you like a little heat you can always add more curry powder.

Serves 6 as a side dish • Preparation 15 mins • Cook 4 hours • Cooker capacity 5 litres

- 1 small sweet potato, cut into chunks
- 5 baby red potatoes, quartered
- 1 kg (2 lb 3 oz) frozen mixed vegetables, such as carrot, beans, broccoli and cauliflower (see note)
- 400 ml (14 oz) can light coconut cream
- 1 tablespoon cornflour (cornstarch)
- 1 teaspoon mild curry powder
- 1 teaspoon ground cumin
- ½ teaspoon ground turmeric

1. Combine the sweet potato, potato and frozen vegetables in the slow cooker.
2. Mix the remaining ingredients and pour over the vegetables.
3. Cover and cook on high for 1 hour, then on low for 3 hours or until the potato is tender. Serve.

NOTES: You can replace the frozen vegetables with the same quantity of fresh ones if you like. Use whatever you have on hand, cut into smallish chunks.

Some slow cookers cook more slowly than others, so use the high setting for longer if the potato is taking a long time to become tender. Keep the size of the potato chunks small, no more than half the size of a golf ball.

If you want a thicker sauce, stir in extra thickening 10 minutes before serving: use a slurry of another 1 tablespoon of cornflour and 1 tablespoon of water.

Garlic Butter Hasselback Potatoes

These indulgent potatoes are the bomb! The fancy presentation lifts your meal to the next level with minimal effort. It's easy to alter the quantities to serve as many people as you like – allow 1 potato, 1 tablespoon of butter and 1 teaspoon of garlic per person.

Serves 4 • Preparation 15 mins • Cook 4–5 hours • Cooker capacity 5 litres

4 large potatoes, skin on
4 heaped teaspoons minced garlic
5 tablespoons butter

1. Make cuts along each potato at 5mm intervals, about two-thirds of the way through (do not cut all the way through to the chopping board). Arrange in the slow cooker, cut side up.

2. Spread a teaspoon of garlic over each potato, then top each one with a tablespoon of butter. Put the remaining 1 tablespoon of butter in the slow cooker too.

3. Cover and cook on low for 4–5hrs or until potatoes are tender, turning gently halfway through cooking.

4. Lift out carefully with an egg flip so as not to break the slices apart. Serve.

Buttermilk Cabbage

My mum used to cook cabbage with milk and butter on the stovetop when I was a child – I have memories of the milk boiling over and burning. There's no chance of that when it's done in the slow cooker! You can even use the leftover milky, buttery cooking liquid in your mashed potato so there's no wastage.

Serves 4 • Preparation 10 mins • Cook 1¾ hours • Cooker capacity 1.5 litres

¼ large green cabbage, thinly sliced
½ cup milk
2 tablespoons butter

1. Combine all the ingredients in the slow cooker. Cover and cook on high for 1 hour 45 minutes.

NOTE: Slow cookers vary, so keep an eye on the cabbage to make sure it's not drying out. If you use a larger slow cooker, you might need to add a little extra milk.

Honey Mustard Potatoes

I'm a sucker for honey with mustard – I just love the pairing of these two ingredients in anything, and these potatoes are no exception. This is a flavour packed side dish that the whole family will enjoy.

Serves 4 • Preparation 10 mins • Cook 2 hours • Cooker capacity 5 litres

500 g (1 lb 2 oz) baby potatoes, quartered
2 tablespoons honey
1 tablespoon wholegrain mustard
1 teaspoon oil
Salt and cracked black pepper, to taste

1. Line the base of the slow cooker with baking paper. Add the remaining ingredients and stir to coat the potatoes well.

2. Cover and cook on high for 2 hours.

Sweet Chilli Butter Broccoli

I came up with this recipe by chance when I was brainstorming ideas for something different to do with broccoli. What a lucky chance that was! My family absolutely loves it, and it's become one of our favourite side dishes – so simple, yet so full of flavour.

Serves 5 • Preparation 10 mins • Cook 1½ hours • Cooker capacity 5 litres

500 g (1 lb 2 oz) broccoli (see note)
3 teaspoons butter
2 tablespoons sweet chilli sauce
Salt and cracked black pepper, to taste

1. Line the base of the slow cooker with baking paper. Add the broccoli. Top with butter and drizzle the sweet chilli sauce over the top. Season with salt and pepper.

2. Cover and cook on low for 1½ hours.

NOTES: I use frozen broccoli, but fresh is fine – just cut it into small florets to ensure it cooks in the same time.

I use sugar-free sweet chilli sauce to keep the recipe low-carb, but any type you like is fine.

You can always adjust the cooking time if you like your broccoli crisper or softer. I found this time perfect in my 5 litre slow cooker.

Sweet Potato Bake

Many people love a good potato bake, but have you ever tried a sweet potato bake? Once you make this one, you'll wonder why you haven't been using sweet potato all along.

Serves 4 • Preparation 15 mins • Cook 2 hours 20 mins • Cooker capacity 1.5 litres

1 extra-large or 2 medium sweet potatoes, sliced
1 brown onion, thinly sliced
200 ml (6½ fl oz) cooking cream
3 tablespoons sweet chilli sauce
20 g (¾ oz) French onion soup mix (about half a packet)
1½ cups grated tasty cheese

1. Arrange the sweet potato and onion in layers in the slow cooker, filling it almost to the top.

2. Combine the cream, sweet chilli sauce, soup mix and ½ cup cheese. Pour the mixture over the sweet potato.

3. Cover and cook on low for 2 hours or until almost tender (not mushy).

4. Scatter the remaining cheese on top and cook for another 20 minutes to melt the cheese nicely and finish cooking the potato.

NOTE: There's no need to put a tea towel under the lid for this one.

Basic Vegetables
Slow-cooked Style

A large part of the convenience of slow cooking is having something ready to serve straight from the pot at dinnertime. So why not include all your vegetables right alongside your main course and have everything ready to go! Wrapping them tightly in foil is the key – it allows you to cook your vegies alongside your main meal while keeping them firm and intact. As well as cooking root vegetables, you can cook softer things such as zucchini, beans, squash and broccoli – allow ½–1 cup per parcel. To cook potatoes, pierce the skin with a skewer a few times to allow the seasoning to penetrate.

Serves as many as you need • Preparation 10 mins • Cook according to vegetable and slow cooker size

Vegetables of your choice, peeled if necessary, cut into uniform size pieces
Salt, freshly ground black pepper, fresh or dried herbs or seasoning of your choice
1 teaspoon butter per parcel

1. Tear foil into 20 x 20 cm (8 x 8 inch) squares, allowing two squares per parcel.
2. Arrange vegetables on foil and add seasoning and a teaspoon of butter. Wrap tightly to form a well-sealed parcel.
3. Wrap the parcel in a second piece of foil, pressing firmly to seal. Put the parcels in the slow cooker with the main meal, occasionally checking whether the vegetables are cooked during cooking time.

NOTES: Cooking times for this method vary, and the best thing you can do is test your vegetables at intervals to see if they are cooked. Timing will vary based on several factors:
- the size of the vegetable pieces and the size of the parcels
- the type of vegetable – potatoes may take 4 hours, while broccoli may take only 1 hour
- the size of your slow cooker. What takes 3 hours in my 1.5 litre (6 cup) cooker, which cooks fairly 'hot', would need longer in my 3 litre (12 cup) cooker; but my 6.5 litre (26 cup) cooker runs much hotter again, so getting to know your cooker involves some trial and error.
- what else is in the cooker. Vegetables will cook faster on their own than if sharing the slow cooker with another dish, and of course it depends on whether the other dish is cooking on high or low.

Cheesy Potato Smash

This is a good option for a potato side dish at your next barbecue. The recipe will easily serve six but could be halved or even doubled. It's great with a sizzling steak and a side salad, and it's easy to serve directly from the slow cooker.

Serves 6 • Preparation 10 mins • Cook 3½ hours • Cooker capacity 7 litres

4 large potatoes, skin on, cut into 2 cm (¾ inch) cubes
2 tablespoons diced bacon
1 small onion, diced
2 tablespoons butter
Cracked black pepper, to taste
1 cup grated tasty cheese

1. Put the potatoes in a single layer in the slow cooker. Scatter the bacon and onion over the top and dot with butter. Season with cracked black pepper.

2. Cover and cook on high for 3¼ hours, or until the potato is tender but not too soft.

3. Scatter the cheese over the potato and cook for another 15 minutes or until the cheese is melted.

4. Serve straight from your slow cooker – delicious!

Garlic Butter Mushrooms

If you love mushrooms as much as I do, you could eat these on their own. The mushrooms become infused with a delicious garlic flavour. This recipe can easily be doubled or increased to serve as many people as you wish.

Serves 3–6 • Preparation 5 mins • Cook 1 hour • Cooker capacity 1.5 litres

6 large flat mushrooms
1 teaspoon butter
1–2 garlic cloves, minced

1. Brush or peel the mushrooms, if you like. I like to leave the skin on. Put the mushrooms top side down in a slow cooker. Add the butter and as much garlic as you like.
2. Cover and cook on high for 1 hour, stirring occasionally if you like, but you don't really need to.
3. Serve the mushrooms drizzled with the garlic butter.

Honey Carrots

Why have boring carrots when you could have these tasty honey carrots? This is an easy way to jazz up a sometimes ordinary vegetable.

Serves 5 • Preparation 5 mins • Cook 2 hours • Cooker capacity 1.5 litres

4 carrots, sliced
3 tablespoons honey
2 tablespoons butter
2 tablespoons light brown sugar
Juice of ½ a small lemon
2 teaspoons sesame seeds

1. Put the carrot in the slow cooker. Add the honey, butter, sugar and lemon juice. Stir to combine.

2. Cover and cook on high for 2 hours, or until the carrots are tender. Drain and reserve the cooking liquid.

3. Place the carrots in a serving bowl and spoon 2–3 tablespoons of the reserved liquid over the top. Sprinkle with sesame seeds and serve.

Cheesy Broccoli and Cauliflower Stuffed Potatoes

You've no doubt tasted a stuffed potato. You've probably enjoyed broccoli and cauliflower in cheese sauce too. But have you ever had cheesy broccoli and cauliflower stuffed inside a potato boat? These are so good! They look amazing too, so they're a worthy addition to your next dinner party. People will assume you've gone to a lot of trouble, but this slow cooker recipe is as easy as can be.

Serves 5 • Preparation 20 mins • Cook 4¼ hours • Cooker capacity 6 litres

5 large potatoes, skin on
2 cups mixed frozen broccoli and cauliflower, thawed and chopped into small
    pieces
1 sachet instant cheese sauce mix
½ cup grated extra-sharp parmesan cheese

1. Place the whole potatoes in the slow cooker and cook on high for 3 hours or until tender when tested with a fork.

2. Meanwhile, soak the broccoli and cauliflower in a bowl of boiling water for 5 minutes. Drain and set aside.

3. Cut the potatoes in half lengthways. Scoop out the centres with a teaspoon, leaving at least 5 mm (¼ inch) of flesh all round so the potatoes hold their shape. (Use the potato you remove for something else.)

4. Fill the potato halves with broccoli and cauliflower. Line the slow cooker with baking paper and add the filled potatoes.

5. Make the cheese sauce according to the directions on the packet. Spoon the sauce over the potatoes. Top with parmesan.

6. Cover, putting a tea towel (dish towel) under the lid, and cook on high for 1¼ hours, until the vegetables are heated through and the cheese is melted.

Honey-Mustard Corn Cobs

We eat a lot of fresh corn on the cob in our house. This recipe gives a lovely sweet touch to fresh corn and really lifts it.

Serves 1 cob per person (or half each if large cobs) • **Preparation** 10 mins
• **Cook** 1½ hours • **Cooker capacity** 7 litres

Corn cobs, husks and fibrous hairs removed
1 teaspoon wholegrain mustard per cob
1 teaspoon butter per cob
1 teaspoon honey per cob

1. Place a rectangular sheet of foil on the benchtop and place a corn cob on top.
2. Spread mustard on each cob, then top with butter and drizzle the honey over.
3. Fold the foil around the corn to form parcels. Place in the slow cooker.
4. Cover and cook on high for 1½ hours. Open the parcels and turn the corn over halfway through the cooking time. (Be careful when opening the foil, as steam will escape.)
5. Serve the corn drizzled with the honey-mustard juices.

Creamy Potato Bake with Chorizo and Bacon

I love a good potato bake. It's such a great side dish for a barbecue or any number of main meals. Think of this as the loaded potato bake of your dreams – the chorizo and bacon give it so much flavour and the creamy cheesy sauce is to die for. If your budget is tight, you can replace the chorizo with more bacon, but personally I find it a worthwhile expense for the taste it delivers.

Serves 6 • Preparation 15 mins • Cook 4½ hours • Cooker capacity 5 litres

Spray oil
850 g (1 lb 14 oz) small potatoes, skin on, thinly sliced
1 small brown onion, thinly sliced
100 g (3½ oz) diced bacon
100 g (3½ oz) chorizo sausage, diced
2 cups cooking cream
2 teaspoons minced garlic
½ teaspoon cracked black pepper
1½ cups grated tasty cheese
Sprinkle of paprika

1. Spray the slow cooker bowl lightly with oil. Arrange half the potato in the slow cooker. Add the onion, bacon and chorizo. Cover with the remaining potatoes.

2. Combine the cream, garlic and pepper and pour over the potatoes.

3. Cover, putting a tea towel (dish towel) under the lid, and cook on high for 2 hours, then on low for 2 hours.

4. Scatter the cheese over the potato and sprinkle with paprika. Replace the tea towel and lid and cook for a further 30 minutes, or until the cheese melts. Serve straight from slow cooker.

NOTES: If your slow cooker has an auto function, use that and cook for 4½ hours.
The paprika on top gives the look of browning, but you can finish the dish in the oven if you prefer.

Cheesy Broccoli and Cauliflower Bake

There is something so yummy about broccoli and cauliflower covered with a lovely cheesy sauce. It's old-style comfort food, great to serve at a barbecue or as a side dish. I cook this in the serving dish so that I can deliver it straight to the table. You could use broccoli or cauliflower alone instead of in combination if you prefer.

Serves 5 • Preparation 15 mins • Cook 1¾ hours • Cooker capacity 7 litres (or whatever fits your serving dish)

500 g (1 lb 2 oz) frozen mixed broccoli and cauliflower (see note)
200 ml (7 fl oz) cooking cream
1 cup grated tasty cheese
1 cup grated mozzarella cheese

1. Pour about 2.5 cm (1 inch) warm water into the slow cooker. Make sure the water level is not so high that it could flow into your serving dish when it is placed in the water bath.

2. Place the broccoli and cauliflower in a heatproof serving dish. Mix the cream with the tasty cheese and pour over the vegetables.

3. Carefully lower the dish into the water in your slow cooker.

4. Cover, putting a tea towel (dish towel) under the lid, and cook on high for 1½ hours or until the vegetables are tender.

5. Scatter the mozzarella cheese over the vegetables and cook for another 15 minutes or until the mozzarella has melted.

6. Lift the serving dish carefully out of the slow cooker bowl.

NOTE: I use frozen vegetables, but fresh are fine – just cut the broccoli and cauliflower into florets.

Brussels Sprouts with Bacon

Lovely tender Brussels sprouts with bacon and a hint of garlic.

Serves 4 • Preparation 5 minutes • Cook 3 hours • Cooker capacity 1.5 litres

300g (10½ oz) Brussels sprouts
100g (3½ oz) diced bacon
2 cups chicken stock
2 teaspoons minced garlic
Butter (optional), to serve

1. Place all the ingredients in the slow cooker.

2. Cover and cook on low for 3 hours or until the sprouts are tender.

3. Divide the sprouts between serving plates and add a small knob of butter to each serve, if you like.

Baked Baby Potatoes

You can use these to make a potato salad, or serve them as a side dish. Our kids like them cut open with a dollop of butter or sauce on top (you know what kids are like with their sauce!).

Serves 5 • Preparation 5 mins • Cook 3 hours • Cooker capacity 6 litres

10 baby potatoes
1–2 tablespoons olive oil
2 teaspoons chopped chives
1 teaspoon chopped fresh parsley

1. Place the potatoes in the slow cooker. Drizzle with olive oil and season with salt and pepper.

2. Cover and cook on low for 3 hours or until tender.

3. Remove from slow cooker and place in a bowl. Add the fresh herbs and season with more salt and pepper if you like. Toss to coat.

NOTE: If you use larger potatoes you will need to increase the cooking time.

INTERNATIONAL FLAVOURS

Mee Goreng

I love mee goreng from an Asian restaurant – it's one of my favourites – so naturally I set out to re-create it at home with the slow cooker. This is just like having a takeaway at home, and for a fraction of the cost. The flavour of the garnish really completes it.

Serves 2 • Preparation 20 mins • Cook 2¾–3¼ hours • Cooker capacity 5 litres

1½ tablespoons sesame oil
500 g (1 lb 2 oz) chicken thigh fillets, sliced into strips
2 tablespoons minced ginger
1 tablespoon minced garlic
½ cup chicken stock
¼ cup kecap manis (sweet soy sauce)
¼ cup sweet chilli sauce
1 tablespoon soy sauce
1 tablespoon cornflour (cornstarch), mixed to a slurry with 1 tablespoon water
440 g (15½ oz) packet fresh thin egg noodles
1 cup bean sprouts
2 spring onions (scallions), thinly sliced, plus extra to garnish
Crisp fried shallots, to garnish

1. Heat the sesame oil in the searing insert of a slow cooker or a frying pan over medium–high heat. Add the chicken, ginger and garlic and fry for about 5 minutes, until the chicken is browned. Transfer the chicken (or the insert) to the slow cooker.

2. Add the chicken stock, kecap manis, sweet chilli sauce and soy sauce. Cover, reduce the heat to low and cook for 2½–3 hours, until the chicken is very tender.

3. Stir in the cornflour slurry, then add the noodles and cook for 10 minutes to heat through.

4. Add the bean sprouts and spring onion and cook for 5 minutes.

5. Serve garnished with extra spring onion and fried shallots.

NOTE: You'll find packets of crisp fried shallots in the Asian section at the supermarket.

Mexican Sausages

The whole family will love these fast and simple sausages.

Serves 6 • Preparation 10 mins • Cook 5 hours • Cooker capacity 5 litres

12 thin beef sausages
1 large onion, thinly sliced
1 green capsicum (pepper) diced
120 g (4 oz) can corn kernels, drained
400 g (14 oz) can diced tomatoes
50 g (1¾ oz) packet Mexican burrito seasoning
Brown rice or mashed potato, to serve

1. Place the sausages in the slow cooker and top with the onion, capsicum and corn.

2. Combine the tomatoes, 2 cups water and burrito seasoning and pour the mixture over the sausages.

3. Cover and cook on low for 5 hours.

4. Serve with brown rice or mashed potato.

Chicken Laksa

This is a mild laksa the whole family can enjoy, without the price tag of a takeaway. The smell while it's cooking is amazing. It might bring the neighbours knocking – you've been warned!

Serves 4 • Preparation 20 mins • Cook 5 hours 10 mins • Cooker capacity 5 litres

500 g (1 lb 2 oz) chicken breast fillets, cubed
2 cups chicken stock
400 ml (14 fl oz) can light coconut milk
1 red capsicum (pepper), sliced
1 red onion, thinly sliced
3 tablespoon laksa paste
2 tablespoons cornflour (cornstarch)
1 tablespoon minced ginger
1 tablespoon soy sauce
1 tablespoon fish sauce
1 tablespoon brown sugar
1 tablespoon shredded kaffir lime leaves
2 cups bean sprouts
40 g (1½ oz) dried vermicelli rice noodles
1 cup thinly sliced spring onions (scallions)

1. Combine all the ingredients except the bean sprouts, noodles and spring onion in the slow cooker. Cover and cook on low for 5 hours.

2. Break up the noodles and add them to the slow cooker. Cook for another 5–10 minutes, until the noodles are tender.

3. Divide between serving bowls, and top each bowl with bean sprouts and spring onion.

NOTE: I would call this laksa mild to medium in terms of heat. If you like yours hot, use extra laksa paste or add some diced chilli.

Singapore Noodles with Chicken, Prawns and Chinese Barbecue Pork

I love Singapore noodles, but who can afford the takeaway version? This is just as good for a fraction of the price, and you can vary the meat and seafood to suit your taste. I purchase the Chinese barbecue pork in slices from the supermarket deli counter.

Serves 2 • Preparation 20 mins • Cook 1½ hours • Cooker capacity 5 litres

1 chicken thigh fillet, thinly sliced
1 onion, thinly sliced
2 tablespoons soy sauce
1 tablespoon mirin
1 tablespoon sake
2 teaspoons sesame oil
2 teaspoons curry powder
2 teaspoons minced garlic
1 teaspoon minced ginger
1 teaspoon brown sugar
¼ teaspoon ground white pepper
4 eggs, whisked
1 red capsicum (pepper), thinly sliced
100 g (3½ oz) Chinese barbecue pork, sliced
6 large raw prawns (shrimp), peeled
125 g (4½ oz) dried rice vermicelli noodles
1 cup hot chicken stock

1. Combine the chicken, onion, soy sauce, mirin, sake, sesame oil, curry powder, garlic, ginger, sugar and white pepper in the slow cooker. Cover and cook on high for 45 minutes or until the chicken is cooked through.

2. Meanwhile, cook the egg for 3–4 minutes in a nonstick frying pan on the stovetop, turning once, to make an omelette. (Alternatively, cook it on a large plate in the microwave.) Cool, slice into ribbons, cover and set aside in the refrigerator.

3. Add the capsicum and pork to the slow cooker and cook for 15 minutes.

4. Stir in the green prawns, add the noodles, then pour in the hot chicken stock. Cook for 30 minutes, stirring every 10 minutes to loosen the cakes of noodles and combine them with the other ingredients.

5. Gently stir in the sliced omelette, then serve.

Super Simple Chicken Tikka Masala

I admit I'm a fairly recent convert to Indian food, but now that I've found it, I wish I hadn't wasted so much time. Yum yum yum! This mild chicken curry hits the spot. It's perfect for young and old alike, but if you like it hotter, just increase the amount of curry paste to ½ cup or to suit your taste.

Serves 4 • Preparation 10 mins (plus marinating) • Cook 4–5 hours • Cooker capacity 5 litres

    750 g (1 lb 10½ oz) chicken thigh fillets
    ½ cup natural yoghurt
    ⅓ cup tikka masala paste (you must use a paste, not a cooking sauce)
    400 g (14 oz) can tomato purée
    300 ml (10 fl oz) cooking cream
    Steamed rice, to serve

1. Combine the chicken, yoghurt and tikka masala paste in a bowl, cover and refrigerate to marinate. Leave it overnight if possible, but for at least a few hours.

2. Transfer the chicken mixture to the slow cooker and stir in the tomato purée and cream.

3. Cover and cook on low for 4–5 hours or until the chicken is very tender.

4. Serve on steamed rice.

NOTES: I like to shred the chicken fillets towards the end of the cooking time and return them to the sauce. This gives a thicker, creamier result.

Beef and Black Bean

This classic Asian dish is the one my husband always orders if we're lucky enough to dine out at a Chinese restaurant. Of course I had to create my own slow-cooked version for him. Serve this with rice or fried rice for a great takeaway-style meal at a fraction of the cost.

Makes 2 large serves • Preparation 15 mins • Cook 2½ hours • Cooker capacity 5 litres

500 g (1 lb 2 oz) beef stir-fry strips
2 cups frozen broccoli florets
1 large onion, cut into thin wedges
1 red capsicum (pepper), cut into strips
2 teaspoons minced ginger
1 teaspoon minced garlic
⅓ cup black bean sauce

1. Combine all the ingredients in the slow cooker. Cover and cook on high for 2½ hours.
2. Serve with or without rice.

NOTE: Add the broccoli 1 hour into the cooking time if you like it slightly crisp. My children prefer it soft, so I add it at the start.

Mild Thai Chicken and Mango Curry

This recipe blends several classics I love: think mango chicken, but with a Thai curry twist. It's mild enough for the whole family to enjoy. Serve with rice and vegetables.

Serves 5 • Preparation 15 mins • Cook 4 hours • Cooker capacity 5 litres

1 kg (2 lb 3 oz) chicken thigh fillets
1 small onion, diced
1½ cups mango nectar
165 ml (5½ fl oz) can coconut milk
40g (1½ oz) sachet dry French onion soup mix
½ teaspoon curry powder, or to taste
1 tablespoon cornflour (cornstarch), mixed to a slurry with 1 tablespoon water
  (optional)

1. Place the chicken and onion in the slow cooker. Combine all the other ingredients except the cornflour slurry and pour them over the chicken.

2. Cover, putting a tea towel (dish towel) under the lid, and cook on low for 4 hours.

3. Check the thickness of the sauce. If it needs thickening, stir in the cornflour slurry and cook for another 10 minutes. I find that this usually isn't necessary.

San Choy Bow

There's something about a great san choy bow that always has you licking your lips (and your fingers) – am I right? This version is no exception. It's perfect enjoyed as part of a Chinese banquet, or as a meal on its own.

Makes 8 lettuce cups • Preparation 15 mins • Cook 1¾ hours • Cooker capacity 3.5 litres

500 g (1 lb 2 oz) minced (ground) pork
2 tablespoons oyster sauce
1 tablespoon minced ginger
3 teaspoons sesame oil
2 small red chillies, thinly sliced (see note)
2 teaspoons minced garlic
1 cup bean sprouts
½ spring onions (scallions), thinly sliced
8 lettuce leaf cups

1. Combine the pork, oyster sauce, ginger, sesame oil, chilli and garlic in the slow cooker. Cover and cook on high for 1½ hours, then stir well.

2. Add the bean sprouts and spring onion and cook for 15 minutes.

3. Spoon the mixture into lettuce leaf cups and serve.

NOTES: Deseed the chillies if, like me, you don't like your food too spicy. Or leave the seeds in for extra heat.

You could serve the mince on wraps instead of in lettuce leaf cups. With the lettuce option, it's a low-carb meal.

The recipe is easily doubled to serve a crowd.

Teriyaki Beef

I love making my own versions of Asian dishes and adding a little twist. The twist in this recipe is that it uses a mince base instead of the usual steak – and wow, is it yummy! Of course you could use chicken or beef strips instead, and extend the cooking time slightly, or use chicken mince. But do try the beef mince first – you'll be surprised at how amazing it tastes.

Serves 4 • Preparation 10 mins • Cook 5 hours • Cooker capacity 3.5 litres

1 kg (2 lb 3 oz) lean minced (ground) beef
½ cup mirin
½ cup sake
½ cup low-salt soy sauce
¼ cup (firmly packed) brown sugar
1 tablespoon minced ginger
1 tablespoon minced garlic
1 tablespoon cornflour (cornstarch), mixed to a slurry with 1 tablespoon water
Steamed jasmine rice, to serve

1. Combine all the ingredients except the cornflour slurry in the slow cooker. Cover and cook on low for 4½ hours.

2. Skim off and discard any oil that's accumulated on the surface (I use a small measuring cup). If there are any lumps in the mince, use a potato masher to break them up.

3. Stir in the cornflour slurry and cook for another 30 minutes.

4. Serve with steamed jasmine rice.

Must Try Mexican Shredded Beef

Incredibly tasty, this recipe uses just four ingredients – so easy! We serve the beef on bread rolls with slaw, but you could use it in any of your favourite Mexican dishes – tacos, burritos, enchiladas – or on pizza. Hands down, this is one of my favourite Mexican recipes by far.

Serves 6 • Preparation 10 mins • Cook 6 or 9 hours • Cooker capacity 6 litres

1 kg (2 lb 3 oz) piece beef blade roast
50 g (1¾ oz) packet burrito seasoning
440 g (15½ oz) can refried beans
375 g (13 oz) bottle enchilada cooking sauce (see note)

1. Combine all the ingredients in the slow cooker. Cover and cook on high for 6 hours or on low for 9 hours.

2. Remove the meat from the sauce, shred, return it to the slow cooker and stir to coat, then serve.

NOTE: You could use nachos sauce, salsa or canned tomato purée instead of enchilada sauce, but it won't have the same depth of flavour.

⟾ Thai Peanut Chicken ⟶

Fresh lime juice cuts through the beautiful Thai flavours in this dish. Serve the chicken with brown rice and green vegetables.

Serves 6 • Preparation 5 mins • Cook 4 hours • Cooker capacity 5 litres

1 kg (2 lb 3 oz) chicken thigh fillets
¾ cup chunky tomato salsa
⅓ cup peanut butter (smooth or crunchy)
2 tablespoons lime juice
1 tablespoon soy sauce
1 teaspoon minced ginger
⅓ cup coarsely chopped peanuts
Brown rice, steamed Asian greens and lime wedges, to serve

1. Put the chicken in the slow cooker.

2. Combine the salsa, peanut butter, lime juice, soy sauce and ginger in a small bowl. Pour the mixture over the chicken. Cover and cook on low for 4 hours.

3. Divide between bowls and scatter with peanuts. Add a lime wedge and serve with brown rice and Asian greens.

Loaded Spanish Bake

Think of this as a Spanish potato bake with one of my favourite combinations: chicken and chorizo. It's a one-pot meal everyone can enjoy. If you have little children who might find chorizo too spicy, you can leave it out.

Serves 5 • Preparation 10 mins • Cook 5 hours 15 mins • Cooker capacity 6 litres

Spray oil
5 potatoes, skin on, thinly sliced
400 g (14 oz) can diced tomatoes
2 teaspoons minced garlic
1 teaspoon dried oregano
2 teaspoons chicken stock powder
1 red onion, sliced
400 g (14 oz) chicken breast fillet
125 g (4½ oz) chorizo sausage, sliced
3 eggs

1. Spray the slow cooker bowl with oil and arrange the potato on the base. Combine the tomatoes, garlic and oregano and pour over the potato. Sprinkle with chicken stock powder, then spread the onion slices over.

2. Cut the chicken breast in half lengthways, then slice each half into thin strips. Spread the chicken slices over the onions, then arrange the chorizo slices over the chicken.

3. Cover and cook on high for 5 hours.

4. Make 3 indentations in the top of the ingredients and crack an egg into each one. Cover and cook for about another 15 minutes, until the eggs have set.

Slow-cooked Mexican Taco Mince

This recipe was created for those who like to avoid packets and pre-made ingredients. Why buy taco seasoning when you can make your own with a simple mix of spices? This recipe makes a flavour-packed mince to serve with tacos, burritos or any other Mexican dish you like. Use lean mince for a low-fat option.

Serves 8 • Preparation 10 mins • Cook 2 or 4 hours • Cooker capacity 1.5 litres

1 kg (2 lb 3 oz) lean minced (ground) beef
¼ cup hot water
1½ teaspoon chilli flakes
1 teaspoon ground cumin
1 teaspoon paprika
1 teaspoon garlic powder
½ teaspoon onion powder
½ teaspoon dried oregano

1. Heat a little oil in the searing insert of a slow cooker or a frying pan over medium–high heat. Add the mince and cook until browned. Transfer to the slow cooker.

2. Add the remaining ingredients and stir to combine.

3. Cover and cook on high for 2 hours or on low for 4 hours. Stir occasionally if you're nearby.

NOTE: This is about as spicy as mince made with regular store-bought taco seasoning, so it's child friendly. Increase the chilli if you like more heat.

Asian-inspired Whole Chicken

I love chicken, everything chicken! And Asian is my favourite international fare, so it was only to be expected that I would try to combine the two. The result was this delicious recipe for a whole chicken. It's lovely served with a crunchy Asian salad.

Serves 4–6 • Preparation 5 mins • Cook 6 hours • Cooker capacity 6 litres

1 large chicken (about 2.5 kg/5½ lb)
½ cup soy sauce
¼ cup (firmly packed) light brown sugar
3 tablespoons finely diced ginger
5 garlic cloves, minced
2 teaspoons sesame oil
1 teaspoon cracked black pepper

1. Put the chicken in the slow cooker, breast-side down.
2. Combine the remaining ingredients in a bowl and pour over the chicken.
3. Cover and cook on low for 6 hours. If you're around, spoon the juices over the chicken every hour or so. This will help to achieve a rich colour by the end of cooking.

NOTE: A smaller chicken will require a shorter cooking time.

Thai Chicken and Prawn Yellow Curry (Gaeng Karee)

I created this dish in the early days of my interest in Thai cooking, and it remains hands-down my favourite Thai dish to cook. It's not too spicy for little ones, but you can reduce the heat by adding less curry paste. This is lovely served with a side of basmati rice. If you don't like seafood, leave out the prawns.

Serves 6 • Preparation 15 mins • Cook 4 hours • Cooker capacity 5 litres

1 teaspoon olive oil
700 g (1 lb 9 oz) skinless chicken thigh fillets, diced
⅓ cup Thai yellow curry paste
400 ml (13½ fl oz) can light coconut milk
1 large onion, cut into thin wedges
1 red capsicum (pepper), sliced
1 heaped tablespoon light brown sugar
2 baby pak choy, bases trimmed
12 snow peas (mange tout), trimmed
14 medium raw prawns (shrimp), peeled and deveined, tails left on
1 tablespoon cornflour (cornstarch), mixed to a slurry with 1 tablespoon water (optional)

1. Heat the oil in the searing insert of a slow cooker or a frying pan over medium–high heat. Add the chicken and cook for about 5 minutes, until browned. Add the curry paste and cook, stirring, for 3 minutes, until fragrant. Transfer to the slow cooker.

2. Add the coconut milk, onion, capsicum and brown sugar and stir to combine.

3. Cover and cook on high for 1 hour then on low for 2½ hours.

4. Add the pak choy, snow peas and prawns. Stir to combine and cook for 15 minutes.

5. Check the thickness of the sauce. If it's too watery, stir in the cornflour slurry.

6. Cook for another 15 minutes.

Thai Green Chicken Curry

I'm a relatively new convert to Thai food, but green chicken curry is my go-to order if I'm ever unsure what to choose at a Thai restaurant. This version is mild enough for the whole family to enjoy, but incorporates the Thai flavours you want. It's a great option for entertaining or when you want to enjoy the taste of take-away made at home.

Serves 6 • Preparation 20 mins • Cook 6 hours • Cooker capacity 5 litres

1 kg (2 lb 3 oz) skinless chicken thigh fillets
100 g (3½ oz) green beans, trimmed and halved
½ eggplant, cubed
½ green capsicum (pepper), cut into strips
2 kaffir lime leaves, thinly sliced
1 tablespoon fish sauce
1 tablespoon lime juice
800 ml (27 fl oz) coconut milk
⅓ cup Thai green curry paste
1 tablespoon cornflour (cornstarch)
1 bunch broccolini, trimmed, cut into florets
1 zucchini, halved and sliced
1 bunch buk choy, trimmed
60 g (2 oz) baby spinach leaves
Lime wedges, to serve

1. Combine the chicken, beans, eggplant, capsicum, lime leaves, fish sauce and lime juice in the slow cooker. Whisk the coconut milk, curry paste and cornflour together and add to the slow cooker.

2. Cover and cook on low for 4½ hours.

3. Add the broccolini and zucchini and cook for 30 minutes.

4. Add the buk choy and spinach and cook for a further 1 hour.

5. Serve with fresh lime wedges for a beautiful Thai taste.

Spanish Chicken

This recipe may be best suited to the older children and adults of your house. For little people, we leave out the chorizo and olives when serving and they still enjoy this dish with the family. It's a great low-carb recipe for anyone watching their carb intake.

Serves 6 • Preparation 20 mins • Cook 5½ hours • Cooker capacity 6 litres

1 chorizo sausage, halved lengthways then sliced
1 red onion, sliced
2 teaspoons olive oil
1.5 kg (3 lb 5 oz) chicken drumsticks
400 g (14 oz) can cherry tomatoes in juice
1 red capsicum (pepper), sliced
½ cup chicken stock
2 teaspoons smoked paprika
100 g (3½ oz) mixed green and black pitted olives
Couscous, to serve

1. Sear the chorizo and onion in the olive oil in a searing slow cooker or frying pan for 5–10 minutes or until golden brown. Combine in the slow cooker with all the ingredients except the olives.

2. Cover and cook on low for 5 hours.

3. Add the olives and cook for a further 30 minutes. Serve with couscous

Easy Chow Mein

This is a great budget friendly meal the whole family can enjoy: mince, vegetables, noodles and egg with tasty Asian flavours. Kids can help cook this, and they'll like eating it too.

Serves 4 • Preparation 15 mins • Cook 4 hours 35 mins • Cooker capacity 6 litres

1 kg (2 lb 3 oz) minced (ground) beef
2 tablespoons low-salt soy sauce
1 heaped teaspoon minced garlic
1 heaped teaspoon minced ginger
1 teaspoon sesame oil
350 g (12½ oz) slaw mix (shredded cabbage, carrot, celery and red onion)
½ cup sliced spring onions (scallions), plus extra to garnish (optional)
2 x 70 g (2½ oz) packets 2-minute noodles (I use mi goreng flavour)
4 eggs, whisked

1. Combine the mince, soy sauce, garlic, ginger and sesame oil in the slow cooker.

2. Cover and cook on low for 4 hours, stirring occasionally to break up any lumps.

3. Add the slaw mix, the spring onions and one of the flavour sachets from the instant noodles. Cover and cook on low for a further 30 minutes.

4. Towards the end of this time, cook the instant noodles as per instructions, using only the one remaining seasoning sachet. Drain the seasoned cooking water and add the noodles to the slow cooker. Cook for 5 minutes, then divide between serving bowls.

5. Meanwhile, scramble the eggs in a saucepan or frying pan. Alternatively, microwave them for 3–4 minutes in a large bowl until set. Carefully slice the scrambled eggs into strips. Top each serve of chow mein with a few egg strips and garnish with spring onion.

NOTE: You may like to increase the soy sauce or add extra spices (such as chilli), depending on your taste. A sprinkle of curry powder would also be a nice addition. Other types of minced meat work well too.

LAMB

Aussie Lamb Shanks

I created this recipe on Australia Day to celebrate this great land of ours. Nothing is more Aussie than Vegemite, and it gives a lovely depth of flavour to this delicious dish. I went heavy on the rosemary, too, for a real flavour burst, and as a bonus I got the smell of rosemary all through the house while it was cooking – it was amazing!

Serves 6 • Preparation 10 mins • Cook 8–10 hours • Cooker capacity 7 litres

6 lamb shanks
⅓ cup honey
1 tablespoon Vegemite
8–10 rosemary stalks, each about the length of your palm.

1. Place the lamb shanks the slow cooker (if they have plastic sleeves on the ends, be sure to remove them).

2. Combine the honey and Vegemite in a microwave-safe bowl and microwave for 30 seconds, then stir well to combine. Brush the mixture over the shanks to coat them.

3. Lay the rosemary over the shanks (keep the leaves on the stalks so you can easily remove them before serving).

4. Cover and cook until the shanks are very tender: for 8–10 hours on low, or for 2 hours on high then 6 hours on low, or use the auto setting for 8 hours for the same result.

NOTE: Using a 7 litre cooker means the shanks will fit in a single layer, but if you need to stack them that's okay too – just rotate their position halfway through cooking.

Roast Lamb and Gravy Rolls

Classic roast lamb is absolutely delicious served on fresh bread rolls, and this method results in a rich gravy too. It's a great self-serve option for parties.

Serves 8+ • Preparation 5 mins • Cook 8 hours • Cooker capacity 5 litres

1–2 kg (2 lb 3 oz–4 lb 6 oz) boneless lamb rump roast
Salt flakes and cracked black pepper, to taste
2 tablespoons mint sauce
29 g (1 oz) sachet instant gravy powder (I use roast meat flavour)
Soft bread rolls, to serve

1. Place the lamb in the slow cooker and pour the mint sauce over. Season generously with salt and pepper. Cover and cook on low for 8 hours.

2. Remove the lamb, shred the meat and set aside.

3. Measure ¼ cup of the cooking liquid (discard the remainder).

4. Make the instant gravy in a jug following the directions on the packet, but replace ¼ cup boiling water with the reserved cooking liquid.

5. Return the shredded lamb and gravy to the slow cooker and stir to combine.

6. Serve on soft bread rolls.

Lamb Obsession

I stumbled upon this dish by accident by combining a few things I thought would go nicely together. Little did I know it would become my signature dish. I almost never ate lamb before I created this recipe, but we have it pretty much every week in our house now. You can make it using almost any cut of lamb – chops, steaks, leg, shanks, diced or even minced – because all lamb means obsession! And even the most hardened mushroom-haters swear they can't taste the mushrooms. I even use this recipe with beef and chicken, omitting the mint. Even if you don't like mint – I admit I don't – try it here because it adds a perfect little zing to the lamb.

Serves 4–6 • Preparation 5 mins • Cook 6 hours • Cooker capacity 5 litres

6–8 lamb chops, or 2 kg (4 lb 6 oz) of another lamb cut of your choice
1 onion, diced
420 g (15 oz) can condensed cream of mushroom soup
40 g (1½ oz) packet dry French onion soup mix
1–2 tablespoons Worcestershire sauce
1 tablespoon mint sauce or mint jelly
Mashed potato and steamed vegetables, to serve

1. Put the lamb in the slow cooker. Scatter the onion over the lamb. Combine the mushroom soup, French onion soup mix, Worcestershire sauce and mint sauce or jelly in a bowl and pour the mixture over the lamb. Cover and cook on low for 6 hours for chops or up to 8 hours for a large leg of lamb.

2. Serve the lamb with the cooking sauce, mashed potato and steamed vegetables.

Sweet Lamb Curry

This dish came about when I was handing out meals to patients at my work, including a sweet lamb curry. It smelled so good! I'd never even eaten one before because I don't usually like fruit in cooked meals, but I set myself the challenge to make one of my own, and the minute I tasted it I was hooked! After 'lamb obsession' (page 103), this is my second-favourite slow-cooked meal of all time. We have it regularly in our house and it's not too spicy for all the family to enjoy – even my toddler loves it. We serve it with creamy mashed potato or rice and crusty bread rolls to mop up all the delicious sauce.

Serves 6 • Preparation 5 mins • Cook 5 hours • Cooker capacity 5 litres

1 kg (2 lb 3 oz) diced lamb (I have a butcher debone and dice a leg piece)
1 large onion, diced
2 small green cooking apples, peeled, cored and diced
½ cup beef stock
½ cup fruit chutney
3 teaspoon mild curry powder
2 garlic cloves, minced
½ teaspoon minced ginger
2–3 tablespoons cornflour (cornstarch), mixed to a slurry with 2–3 tablespoons
   water

1. Put all the ingredients except the cornflour in the slow cooker and stir well to combine.

2. Cover and cook on high for 2 hours then low for 2½ hours, or on auto for 4½ hours. (If you're not around to adjust the temperature, just start on low and cook for 6½ hours or more.)

3. Stir in the cornflour slurry. Leave the lid slightly askew to help the sauce to thicken, and cook for another 30 minutes.

➡ Slow-cooked 'Roast' Lamb ➡

Simply nothing comes close to this slow-cooked roast lamb with the classic flavours of rosemary and garlic. You can cook vegies alongside the meat if you like, and hey presto, dinner is done.

Serves 6–8 • Preparation 10 Mins • Cook 6–8 hours • Cooker capacity 6 litres

1–2 kg (2 lb 4 oz–4 lb 8 oz) lamb roast, bone-in or boneless
2–3 garlic cloves, halved lengthways
4–6 sprigs rosemary
Vegetables of your choice (optional)
2 teaspoons beef stock powder
½ cup hot water
1–2 tablespoons mint sauce or 3–4 mint leaves, thinly sliced

1. Using a sharp paring knife, make several slits 1–2 cm (½–¾ inch) deep in the lamb and insert half a garlic clove and a rosemary sprig in each hole. Transfer the lamb to the slow cooker. You can put a layer of vegetables on the base of the slow cooker and put the lamb on top at this point if you like.

2. Put the hot water, mint sauce and stock powder in a bowl and stir to combine. Pour the mixture into the slow cooker around the lamb. Cover and cook on low for 6–8 hours, spooning the juices over the lamb several times during the day if you can.

3. Transfer the lamb to a cutting board and remove the garlic and rosemary sprigs. Make a gravy with the pan juices. Carve the meat and serve with the vegetables and gravy.

Saucy Pulled Lamb and Slaw Sliders

Lamb is great to pull or shred, and this recipe makes an easy weekend dinner. Beef or chicken work well too. Serve it with crunchy slaw and soft bread rolls. So yummy!

Makes 10 sliders • Preparation 5 mins • Cook 8 hours • Cooker capacity 5 litres

1–1.5 kg (2 lb 3 oz–3 lb 5 oz) boneless lamb leg or shoulder roast
400 g (14 oz) can diced or crushed tomatoes
1 small onion, finely diced
¼ cup hoisin sauce
¼ cup sweet chilli sauce
2 tablespoons (firmly packed) light brown sugar
1½ tablespoons fish sauce
1 heaped teaspoon crushed garlic
1 heaped teaspoon minced ginger
1 tablespoon cornflour (cornstarch), mixed to a slurry with 1 tablespoon water
Crunchy slaw and soft bread rolls, to serve

1. Put the lamb in the slow cooker. Combine the remaining ingredients (except the cornflour) in a bowl, then pour the mixture over the lamb.

2. Cover and cook on auto for 7 hours, or on high for 2 hours and then low for 5 hours.

3. Remove the lamb and shred or 'pull' the meat using two forks or tongs.

4. Stir the cornflour slurry into the cooking liquid. Return the shredded lamb to the sauce and continue cooking for 1 hour.

5. To serve, pile the lamb and slaw into soft bread rolls.

Lamb Meatballs with Minted Yoghurt Dressing

I've found that the number-one rule for slow-cooking meatballs is to resist all urges to touch or turn them until they are firm. Then you can do so without breaking them. The minted yoghurt dressing gives a fresh zingy touch to this dish, which is great as a filling party-food option.

Makes 25 meatballs • Preparation 15 mins • Cook 3 hours • Cooker capacity 5 litres

500 g (1 lb 2 oz) minced (ground) lamb
¾ cup fine breadcrumbs
½ onion, grated
1 egg
1 tablespoon finely chopped mint
2 teaspoons crushed garlic
1 teaspoon minced ginger
1 vegetable stock cube
1 cup boiling water

MINTED YOGHURT DRESSING
200 g (7 oz) natural yoghurt
1 tablespoon finely chopped mint
2 teaspoons lemon juice

1. Grease the bowl of a slow cooker.

2. Combine the lamb, breadcrumbs, onion, egg, mint, garlic and ginger in a bowl. Season with salt and pepper. Form the mixture into golf ball–sized balls with your hands and gently place in the slow cooker in a single layer.

3. Dissolve the stock cube in the water, then pour the mixture into the slow cooker.

4. Cover and cook on low for 3 hours. Try not to move or turn the meatballs until they are firm, if at all, so as not to break them. I turn them gently after 2 hours and they remain intact.

5. To make the dressing, combine the ingredients in a small bowl. Drizzle over the meatballs or serve on the side as a dipping sauce.

NOTE: Uncooked meatballs can be prepared the night before and stored in the fridge in a single layer in a sealed container.

Rustic Lamb Casserole

There's something about slow cooked lamb. It's just so tender and juicy. Packing it with vegetables makes a filling, nutritious, one-pot meal to fill the whole family on a small budget. We serve this in bowls with crusty bread rolls for mopping up the sauce. You can cook it for longer on low if you need an all-day recipe.

Serves 8 • Preparation 15 mins • Cook 6 hours • Cooker capacity 6 litres

1 kg (2 lb 3 oz) diced lamb
4–6 small potatoes, skin on, roughly chopped
4 thin carrots, roughly chopped
1½ cups diced pumpkin
1 cup frozen peas
2 cups vegetable stock
2 tablespoons tomato paste (concentrated purée)
2 tablespoons Worcestershire sauce
2 tablespoons mint sauce
1 tablespoon fresh thyme leaves
Crusty bread, to serve

1. Combine all the ingredients in the slow cooker and season with freshly ground black pepper.

2. Cover and cook on high for 6 hours. Stir once or twice during cooking, taking care not to break up the vegetables.

3. Serve with crusty bread.

NOTE: You could cook this on low for 8–10 hours instead.

Roast Lamb with Rosemary Butter and Red Wine Sauce

Rosemary and red wine complement lamb beautifully, and go together to form a lush gravy. The red wine is subtle enough for the whole family to enjoy. We have empty plates all round when we serve this at our house.

Serves 6 • Preparation 10 mins • Cook 5 hours • Cooker capacity 5 litres

1.5 kg (3 lb 5 oz) half leg lamb roast
1½ tablespoons soft butter
1 teaspoon dried or 2 teaspoons fresh rosemary
1 heaped teaspoon minced garlic
¼ teaspoon each salt and cracked black pepper
¾ cup hot water
½ cup red wine, such as shiraz
1 tablespoon vegetable stock powder
1 tablespoon tomato paste (concentrated purée)
1 tablespoon cornflour (cornstarch), mixed to a slurry with 1 tablespoon water

1. Place the lamb in the slow cooker. Combine the butter, rosemary, garlic, salt and pepper and mix well. Spread the butter mixture over the top and sides of the lamb with a spoon.

2. Combine the hot water, wine, stock powder and tomato paste in a jug. Pour into the slow cooker around the lamb, but not over the butter.

3. Cover and cook on high for 5 hours. Baste the meat with the cooking juices occasionally if you are around.

4. Remove the lamb from the slow cooker and set aside. Skim and discard the excess fat from the liquid in the slow cooker, then stir in the cornflour slurry. If you have a searing slow cooker, transfer the insert to the stovetop and reduce and thicken the sauce over medium heat. Alternatively, transfer the mixture to a saucepan.

5. Carve the lamb and serve with the gravy.

NOTE: If you're like me and you don't regularly drink wine, you can purchase an inexpensive bottle of shiraz and it will keep for a few months in the fridge – not great for drinking but fine for cooking.

CHICKEN

Taco Chicken

I love chicken. If I could only eat one type of meat for the rest of my life, chicken would be it, so I'm always trying to come up with new ways to cook it. Tasty taco seasoning is a great way to add maximum flavour with minimal effort and cost. The first time I tried to cook this, I had to throw it out after a power outage of several hours left my slow cooker turned off! I was determined to try again, and it was totally worth it in the end.

Serves 4 • Preparation 15 mins • Cook 4 hours • Cooker capacity 5 litres

2 kg (4 lb 6 oz) whole chicken
35 g (1 oz) packet taco seasoning mix
Salad and sour cream (optional), to serve

1. Place the chicken in the slow cooker, breast side down. Pierce the chicken 8–10 times with the tip of a sharp knife.
2. Sprinkle two-thirds of the taco seasoning over the chicken. Rub into the chicken, especially into the cuts. Sprinkle with remaining taco seasoning.
3. Cover and cook on auto for 4 hours. Spoon some of the cooking juices over the chicken 2–3 times during cooking.
4. Serve with salad and a dollop of sour cream (if using).

NOTES: If you don't have an auto setting on your slow cooker, cook on low for 5 hours.

Cooking the chicken with the breast down keeps the breast meat moist.

I use two egg flips to get under each end of the chicken to lift it out when cooked – you could cook it on a trivet or in a chicken sling if you prefer.

⊨— Sweet Chilli BBQ Chicken —●

This juicy full-flavoured chicken is mild enough for the whole family to enjoy. However, if you like it spicier just use a hotter sweet chilli sauce.

Serves 4–6 • Preparation 15 mins • Cook 7 hours • Cooker capacity 6 litres

2 kg (4 lb 6 oz) whole chicken
1 small onion, peeled
½ cup BBQ sauce
⅓ cup sweet chilli sauce
1 teaspoon minced garlic
1 teaspoon minced ginger

1. Place peeled onion inside chicken cavity and place chicken in slow cooker

2. Combine other ingredients and pour over the chicken. Cook on low for 7 hours.

3. Baste with cooking juices several times during cooking for a richer colour.

4. Serve with rice and salad or seasonal side vegetables.

Garlic Butter and White Wine Shredded Whole Chicken

This recipe is a great all rounder. Serve the chicken hot with vegetables or salad for a main meal, or use it in salads or wraps for school lunchboxes. It's tasty but not overpowering, so you can enjoy it on its own or with complementary flavours – on pizza or baked potatoes, for example.

Serves 4 • Preparation 15 mins • Cook 6–7 hours • Cooker capacity 6 litres

1 large or 2 small chickens
2½ tablespoons butter, melted
5–6 garlic cloves, finely diced, or 1 heaped tablespoon minced garlic
1 teaspoon cracked black pepper
1 teaspoon dried rosemary
1 teaspoon dried thyme
½ cup dry white wine

1. Place the chicken in the slow cooker.
2. Combine the butter with all the other ingredients in a small bowl, then pour the mixture over the chicken.
3. Cover and cook on low for 6–7 hours or until the chicken is very tender.
4. Carefully remove the chicken and shred the meat from the bones.

Tropical Chicken

The whole family will love this combination of chicken and pineapple. I've used chicken cutlets, but it would work equally well with drumsticks, wings or thighs.

Serves 6 • Preparation 10 mins • Cook 6 hours • Cooker capacity 5.5 litres

12 skinless chicken thigh cutlets (bone in)
1 tablespoon minced ginger
1 tablespoon chicken stock powder
½ cup teriyaki sauce
440 g (15½ oz) can pineapple pieces, drained
1 tablespoon cornflour (cornstarch), mixed to a slurry with 1 tablespoon water

1. Place the chicken in the slow cooker, spread the ginger over it, and sprinkle with the stock powder. Drizzle the teriyaki sauce over the top, add the pineapple pieces and stir to combine.

2. Cover and cook on low for 6 hours, stirring once during the cooking time if you're around.

3. Carefully remove the chicken and transfer to a bowl. Cover with foil and keep warm.

4. Transfer the searing insert to the stovetop (or transfer the sauce to a saucepan). Stir in the cornflour slurry and cook on high heat for 5 minutes or until the sauce has thickened.

5. Divide the chicken between plates, spoon the sauce and pineapple over and serve.

NOTE: You can reduce the number of chicken pieces if you've got fewer people to feed. This is lovely served with minted peas (page 56) and baked baby potatoes (page 75).

Smoky Maple and barbecue Hasselback Chicken

This recipe combines many of my favourite things: chicken, bacon, cheese, barbecue sauce – what's not to love!? It makes a delicious sauce that's lovely served over creamy mashed potato or rice.

Serves 4 • Preparation 20 mins • Cook 4 hours • Cooker capacity 6 litres

4 large chicken breast fillets
4 rashers maple flavoured streaky bacon
4 slices extra sharp cheddar cheese
1 cup smoky barbecue sauce
1 tablespoon maple syrup
1 teaspoon smoked paprika

1. Make four cuts along each breast fillet, about two-thirds of the way through. Do not cut all the way through to the chopping board. Cut each bacon rasher crossways into 4 pieces, and cut each cheese slice into 4 triangles. Place a piece of bacon and a triangle of cheese into each of the cuts in the chicken.

2. Combine the barbecue sauce, maple syrup and paprika in a small bowl. Pour into the slow cooker. Carefully add the chicken.

3. Cover and cook on low for 4 hours.

4. Serve with as much (or as little) of the cooking sauce as you like.

Chicken and Asparagus Quiche

This quiche is a great way to used up cooked chicken. You can make it ahead of time and pair it with a salad for an easy lunch on the run. It's also lovely with potato gems or wedges. It looks impressive, so it's great to take to social functions too.

Serves 4 • Preparation 20 mins • Cook 2 hours • Cooker capacity 5 litres

Oil spray, for greasing
8 large eggs
200 ml (7 fl oz) cooking cream
1 cup (loosely packed) grated tasty cheese
1 teaspoon salt
½ teaspoon cracked black pepper
14 canned asparagus spears
2 cooked chicken breasts, thinly sliced
½ cup thinly sliced spring onions (scallions)

1. Line the base and sides of the slow cooker with a piece of baking paper. Spray the sides of the slow cooker with oil in case the mixture rises above the paper.

2. Whisk the eggs in a large mixing bowl. Add the cream, cheese, salt and pepper and set aside.

3. Arrange the asparagus spears in the slow cooker to cover the base evenly. Scatter with the chicken, then the spring onion.

4. Pour the egg mixture gently over the top.

5. Cover, putting a tea towel (dish towel) under the lid, and cook on high for 2 hours or until the egg is set.

6. Remove the quiche by lifting out the baking paper. Slice into quarters for a main course or wedges for a party platter and serve.

NOTES: I used a 5 litre slow cooker. You can use a smaller one, but the quiche will be deeper and you will need to extend the cooking time. Cook it until the egg is set.

◼━ Chicken Marsala ━●

This recipe is simple but tastes that little bit fancy, bringing together chicken, mushrooms, a cream-based sauce, and the Italian fortified wine Marsala. If you're concerned about the alcohol content, see the note below. I like to serve this with creamy mashed potato, and carrot and parsnip purée (page 57).

Serves 5 • Preparation 20 mins • Cook 2 hours 10 minutes• Cooker capacity 5 litres

1 kg (2 lb 3 oz) chicken breast fillets, cut into 2.5 cm (1 inch) cubes
1 cup chicken stock
200 g (7 oz) button mushrooms, sliced
½ cup Marsala (see note)
4 garlic cloves, minced
½ teaspoon salt
½ teaspoon cracked black pepper
150 ml (5 fl oz) cooking cream

1. Combine all the ingredients except the cream in the slow cooker. Cover and cook on high for 2 hours.

2. Add the cream and cook for 5–10 minutes or until heated through.

NOTE: Marsala is an Italian fortified wine that's often used in cooking. If you can't find it at your local bottle shop, just ask – it will be shelved separately from the red and white wines. A bottle can cost as little as $10 and will keep for 4–5 months after opening.

Marsala has quite a high alcohol content (15–18%). The slow cooking method doesn't vaporise alcohol as effectively as stovetop cooking. If you're concerned about this, you can boil the wine in a saucepan with the lid off for a few minutes, then let it cool, before you cook with it. This, plus the slow cooking, will take care of most of the alcohol content. Keep in mind that the recipe uses only half a cup, so the amount of alcohol per serve is minimal anyway.

Lemon Chicken

This simple chicken dish with a zesty lemon cream sauce is so tasty the whole family will love it. I know my children did! You'll need two lemons for this recipe – one for zest and two for juice. Before you zest or juice them, reserve a couple of thin slices to use as a garnish.

Serves 4 • Preparation 20 mins • Cook 4 hours 10 minutes • Cooker capacity 5 litres

700 g (1 lb 9 oz) chicken thigh fillets, sliced
¼ cup lemon juice
1 tablespoon butter
2 garlic cloves, minced, or 2 teaspoons minced garlic
2 teaspoons chicken stock powder
Finely grated zest of 1 lemon
150 ml (5 fl oz) cooking cream
1 tablespoon cornflour (cornstarch)
Mashed potato and steamed vegetables, to serve

1. Combine the chicken, lemon juice, butter, garlic, stock powder and lemon zest in the slow cooker. Cover and cook on low for 4 hours or until the chicken is very tender.

2. Whisk the cornflour into the cream, then add to the slow cooker. Stir well and cook for 5–10 minutes or until the sauce has thickened.

3. Serve garnished with a slice of lemon, with mashed potato and steamed vegetables

Chicken Cacciatore

Chicken cacciatore is not only a flavour-packed delight for the tastebuds, but also a bright, colourful feast for the eyes. Combining olives, tomatoes and Italian herbs, it's a lovely addition to your next dinner party menu.

Serves 4 • Preparation 20 mins • Cook 5 hours 10 minutes–6 hours 10 minutes • Cooker capacity 6 litres

8 chicken thigh cutlets, skin on, bone in
400 g (14 oz) can diced Italian tomatoes
1 cup sliced mushrooms
1 red capsicum (pepper), diced
1 large brown onion, diced
½ cup white wine
2 tablespoons tomato paste (concentrated purée)
1 tablespoon minced garlic
3 teaspoons dried Italian herb mix
1 teaspoon cracked black pepper
½ teaspoon salt
16 cherry tomatoes
100 g (3½ oz) green olives (halved or whole, no stuffing)
1 tablespoon cornflour (cornstarch), mixed to a slurry with 1 tablespoon water
Chopped parsley, to garnish
Mashed potato, to serve

1. Place the chicken in the slow cooker. Combine all the other ingredients except the cherry tomatoes, olives, cornflour slurry and parsley in a bowl. Pour the mixture over the chicken.

2. Cover and cook on low for 4–5 hours or until the chicken is very tender.

3. Add the cherry tomatoes and olives and cook for 1 hour.

4. Stir in the cornflour slurry and cook for 10 minutes or until the sauce is thickened.

5. Serve garnished with parsley, with mashed potato.

Supercharged Satay Chicken

There's satay, and then there's SATAY. I love, love, LOVE a good satay, and I wanted this one to have some serious peanut punch to it. This is everything I'd hoped for!

Serves 5 • Preparation 20 mins • Cook 2 hours 40 minutes • Cooker capacity 6 litres

- 1.25 kg (2 lb 12 oz) chicken thigh fillets, sliced into strips
- 1 brown onion, diced
- 1 heaped teaspoon minced garlic
- 270 ml (9 fl oz) can coconut cream
- 1 cup crunchy peanut butter
- ⅓ cup kecap manis (sweet soy sauce)
- 1 tablespoon brown sugar
- 2 teaspoons soy sauce
- 2 teaspoons cornflour (cornstarch)
- 1 teaspoon fish sauce
- 1 small red chilli, deseeded, finely diced
- Steamed brown rice, to serve

1. Cook the chicken, onion and garlic in the searing insert of a slow cooker or a frying pan over medium–high heat for about 5–10 minutes, until the chicken is sealed (there's no need to brown it) and the onion is softened. Transfer the chicken (or the insert) to the slow cooker.

2. Combine the remaining ingredients in a jug and blend with a stick blender until smooth. Pour the mixture over the chicken.

3. Cover, putting a tea towel (dish towel) under the lid. Reduce the heat to low and cook for 2½ hours.

4. Serve on steamed brown rice.

NOTES: This produces a lovely thick satay sauce. You can reduce the peanut butter to ½ cup if you don't like a strong peanut taste, but my family loved it exactly as it was.

You can swap the crunchy peanut butter for smooth if you prefer, and add ⅓ cup crushed peanuts before serving.

One small chilli (without seeds) doesn't make the sauce spicy. Our five year old ate it happily.

Moroccan Poached Chicken
Breast with Garlic

We enjoy a lot of poached chicken in our house. Friendly on the budget and the waistline, it's great to have on hand for sandwiches, pizzas, salads and wraps, and you can serve it with salad for a light meal on a hot day.

Serves 4 • Preparation 10 mins • Cook 1 hour 20 minutes • Cooker capacity 1.5 litres

2 cups warm water
1 tablespoon chicken stock powder
3 teaspoons minced garlic
2 teaspoons Moroccan seasoning
2 medium–large chicken breast fillets

1. Combine the warm water, stock powder, garlic and seasoning in a jug and mix well to dissolve the stock powder. Pour into the slow cooker.

2. Cut each breast fillet horizontally through the middle to make two thinner fillets from each one and add them to slow cooker.

3. Cover and cook on high for 1 hour 20 minutes or until cooked through.

4. Slice thinly and store in an airtight container in the fridge for up to 2 days, or freeze.

Pizza Chicken

Pizza on a dough base is so last year (ha ha). Now imagine your favourite pizza toppings – but on chicken! This will definitely have your kids lining up for seconds.

Serves 6 • Preparation 15 mins • Cook 2–2¼ hours • Cooker capacity 6 litres

6 chicken breast fillets
½ cup tomato paste (concentrated purée)
½ large green capsicum (pepper), thinly sliced
½ red onion, thinly sliced
3 teaspoons dried oregano
50 g (1¾ oz) thinly sliced pepperoni
6 slices smoked cheese or 1 cup grated mozzarella
Salad, to serve

1. Flatten the breast fillets somewhat with a meat mallet. I cover each one with a freezer bag or plastic wrap when I'm doing this to prevent extra mess and splatter.

2. Line the base of the slow cooker with baking paper.

3. Arrange the chicken fillets side by side to fill the base of the cooker in a single layer. Spread the tomato paste over the chicken. Top with capsicum and onion and sprinkle with oregano.

4. Cover, putting a tea towel (dish towel) under the lid, and cook on high for 1½ hours.

5. Top with pepperoni and cheese and cook for 30–45 minutes on high.

6. Serve with salad.

Mango Chutney Chicken Drumsticks

Indian style mango chutney and chicken go together to form a delicious drumstick dinner the whole family can enjoy. With this dish you're just five simple ingredients away from a great meal!

Serves 5-6 • Preparation 15 mins • Cook 5 hours • Cooker capacity 6 litres

1–1½ kg (2 lb 3 oz–3 lb 5 oz) chicken drumsticks
1 onion, diced
425 g (15 oz) can mango, drained and sliced
350 g (12½ oz) jar mango chutney (from the Indian section of the supermarket, not the jam section)
1–2 tablespoons cornflour (cornstarch), mixed to a slurry with 1–2 tablespoons water

1. Put the chicken in the slow cooker and top with the onion. Add the mango and pour over the mango chutney.

2. Cover and cook on low for 4 hours 50 minutes or until the chicken is very tender, stirring halfway through the cooking time.

3. Stir in the cornflour slurry and cook for 10 minutes or until the sauce is thickened to a lovely gravy.

Barbecue Shredded Cheesy Chicken

This is perfect on tortilla wraps, tacos or pizzas, or just served with salad. Draining the liquid partway through cooking stops the chicken from becoming watery and gives the saucy, cheesy finish that works so well in wraps.

Serves 4-6 • Preparation 15 mins • Cook 3¾ hours • Cooker capacity 5 litres

1 kg (2 lb 3 oz) chicken thigh fillets
1 large red onion, sliced
1 tablespoon chicken stock powder
1 cup barbecue sauce
2 cups grated tasty cheese

1. Put the chicken in the slow cooker, sprinkle with the stock powder and top with the onion. Cover and cook on high for 1½ hours.

2. Drain and discard the liquid that forms.

3. Add the barbecue sauce and cook for 2 hours on low.

4. Remove the chicken, shred it, and return it to the sauce. Add the cheese.

5. Cook for 10–15 minutes or until the cheese has melted.

Creamy Tomato and Spinach Chicken Drumsticks

These drumsticks will have you licking your plate clean! This low-carb recipe works well with other cuts of chicken too – thighs or Marylands, for example. I serve it with mashed potato and sweet chilli butter broccoli (page 64).

Serves 6 • Preparation 20 mins • Cook 4–6 hours • Cooker capacity 7 litres

12 chicken drumsticks
2 teaspoons smoked paprika
1 teaspoon cracked black pepper
1 teaspoon onion powder
300 ml (10 fl oz) cooking cream
150 g (5 oz) semidried tomatoes
1 tablespoon minced garlic
1 tablespoon cornflour (cornstarch)
½ cup freshly grated parmesan cheese
60 g (2 oz) baby spinach leaves

1. Put the chicken drumsticks in the slow cooker and sprinkle with the paprika, pepper and onion powder.

2. Combine the cream, tomatoes, garlic and cornflour in a blender and blend until smooth. Pour the mixture over the chicken.

3. Cover, putting a tea towel (dish towel) under the lid, and cook on auto for 4 hours or on low for 5–6 hours, until the chicken is very tender.

4. Transfer the chicken to a bowl and set aside.

5. Whisk the sauce well, then stir in the cheese and spinach.

6. Return the chicken to the slow cooker and coat well with the sauce. Cook for 30 minutes on low.

NOTE: You could halve the number of drumsticks and still make the same amount of sauce.

Chutney Chicken Curry

A fruity, mild, sweet curry, this has just four ingredients, so it's super easy! Pair it with rice or vegetables and enjoy it with the whole family.

Serves 4 • Preparation 15 mins • Cook 5 hours • Cooker capacity 5 litres

1 kg (2 lb 3 oz) chicken thigh fillets
1 onion, diced
2 teaspoons curry powder (see note)
320 g (11 oz) jar fruit chutney

1. Put the chicken in the slow cooker and top with the onion, then sprinkle with curry powder. Add the chutney and stir to combine.

2. Cover and cook on low for 5 hours.

3. Shred the chicken into the sauce, then serve.

NOTES: This is a mild curry, but if you're cooking for little ones, you might want to reduce the curry powder to 1 teaspoon. I use Keen's brand curry powder.

There will be a lot of liquid in the slow cooker after 5 hours, but once you shred the chicken, it will absorb it.

Tomato Pesto Chicken

I really enjoy experimenting with pesto, because it's such an easy way to add stacks of flavour to a recipe. This low-carb dish has just three ingredients – it doesn't get much easier than that!

Serves 2 • Preparation 10 mins • Cook 3–4 hours • Cooker capacity 3.5 litres

400 g (14 oz) chicken fillets, cut into 2.5 cm (1 inch) cubes (I prefer thighs, but breasts are fine too)
200 ml (7 fl oz) cooking cream
100 g (3½ oz) sundried tomato pesto

1. Put the chicken in the slow cooker. Combine the cream and pesto and pour the mixture over the chicken.
2. Cover and cook on low for 3–4 hours or until the chicken is very tender.

NOTES: This recipe could be served with low-carb sides such as broccoli or cauliflower 'rice'. If you enjoy carbs, try it with potatoes, rice or pasta.

Memory Lane Chicken

I named this recipe after my Aunty Muriel. She was like a grandmother to us, and I fondly remember her cooking. One of her favourite dishes in her later years was whole chicken basted with tomato sauce and soy sauce. The flavours stuck with me in my memory and they work perfectly with these slow-cooked chicken pieces too.

Serves 6 • Preparation 10 mins • Cook 5 hours • Cooker capacity 6 litres

2 kg (4 lb 6 oz) chicken drumsticks (see note)
1 cup tomato sauce (ketchup)
¼ cup soy sauce

1. Put the drumsticks in the slow cooker. Combine the sauces and pour them over the chicken.
2. Cover and cook on low for 5 hours.

NOTES: You could use chicken wings, breast fillets or thigh fillets instead of drumsticks. Reduce the cooking time to 3–4 hours depending on your slow cooker.

For a slightly thicker consistency to the sauce, use the tea towel trick: put a tea towel (dish towel) under the lid to catch the condensation that builds up.

⊨—— Apricot Chicken Three Ways ——●

Apricot chicken is a classic recipe and it adapts perfectly to the slow cooker. As well as the traditional version, I've offered two tasty variations here: apricot chicken sausages, and curried apricot chicken.

Serves 4 • Preparation 10 mins • Cook 4 hours • Cooker capacity 5 litres

1 kg (2 lb 3 oz) chicken thigh fillets
1 onion, diced
40g (1½ oz) packet dry French onion soup mix
425 ml (15 fl oz) can apricot nectar or 410 g (14½ oz) can apricot halves in juice,
    or 500 g (1 lb 2 oz) jar apricot jam (jelly)

1. Put the chicken and onion in the slow cooker.
2. Combine the apricot nectar, juice or jam with the soup mix and pour over the chicken. Scatter the apricot halves, if using, over the top.
3. Cover and cook on low for 4 hours.

NOTES: This recipe is very adaptable. Use any cut of chicken – drumsticks work really well. Alternatively, try either of these variations:

For Apricot Chicken Sausages, simply use chicken sausages instead of thigh fillets.

For Curried Apricot Chicken, add 1–2 teaspoons curry powder when you add the onion.

You could also replace the apricot nectar/pieces with a can of mango nectar/pieces in any of these variations.

Brown rice and steamed vegetables make a lovely accompaniment to the classic apricot chicken, though I like to serve the curry with mashed potato and vegetables.

Honey Barbecue Whole Chicken

A whole chicken is great done in the slow cooker. This one uses that magical combination of honey and barbecue sauce to produce a lovely sweet flavour. I like to serve this with salad, slaw, and potato or sweet potato wedges for a great summer meal. Or combine it with steamed or roasted vegetables in cooler weather.

Serves 4 • Preparation 5 mins • Cook 7 hours • Cooker capacity 6 litres

1 large chicken (about 2 kg/4 lb 6 oz)
½ cup honey
½ cup barbecue sauce
¼ cup soy sauce
2 garlic cloves, minced
1 teaspoon mustard powder

1. Place the chicken in the slow cooker.

2. Combine all the other ingredients in a bowl and pour the mixture over the chicken.

3. Cover and cook on low for 7 hours. If you are around, spoon the juices over the chicken every hour or so. This will help to achieve a rich colour by the end of cooking.

4. Carefully lift the chicken out of the slow cooker using tongs and a slotted spoon or egg lifter to keep it from falling apart.

Smoky Barbecue Chicken with Bacon

This recipe brings together two of my favourite flavours: chicken and barbecue-anything, and I'm there! What better to combine with these two flavour powerhouses than bacon? I serve this with mashed potato and steamed vegetables. Be sure to spoon some of the sauce over your potatoes too – so yummy!

Serves 4 • Preparation 10 mins • Cook 4 hours • Cooker capacity 7 litres

Vegetable oil
1 kg (2 lb 3 oz) chicken thigh fillets
250 g (9 oz) bacon, sliced into strips
½ cup barbecue sauce
¼ cup tomato sauce (ketchup)
2 tablespoons Worcestershire sauce
1 tablespoon light brown sugar
1 heaped teaspoon minced garlic
¼ teaspoon paprika
½ teaspoon mustard powder

1. Heat a little oil in the searing insert of a slow cooker or a frying pan over medium–high heat. Add the chicken and bacon and cook until browned. Transfer to the slow cooker.

2. Combine the remaining ingredients in a bowl with ¼ cup water and pour over the chicken and bacon.

3. Cover and cook on low for 4 hours.

Honey Mustard Chicken

This recipe features the traditional honey–mustard flavours that go beautifully with chicken. I like to use thigh fillets when I'm slow-cooking with chicken, but this recipe works with any cut. I serve this with green leafy salad or vegetables.

Serves 4 • Preparation 10 mins • Cook 4 hours • Cooker capacity 5 litres

1 kg (2 lb 3 oz) chicken thigh fillets
4 tablespoons honey
4 tablespoons mild American mustard
1–2 tablespoons cornflour (cornstarch), mixed to a slurry with 2 tablespoons
    water

1. Put the chicken in the slow cooker (don't add anything else at this stage).

2. Cover and cook on low for 2 hours.

3. Remove the chicken and break the fillets into smaller pieces (or leave them whole if you wish). Drain all but ⅓ cup of the chicken juices from the slow cooker. Return the chicken to the slow cooker.

4. Combine the honey and mustard, pour over the chicken and continue cooking for 1¾ hours.

5. Stir in the cornflour slurry and cook for 15 minutes or until the sauce has thickened.

Sticky Teriyaki Chicken

Nothing gets my attention like the words 'sticky' and 'chicken' in the same sentence! I love the flavours in this dish and it's great served with fried rice and steamed broccolini. I've used breast fillets, but you can substitute other cuts.

Serves 4 • Preparation 10 mins • Cook 3¼ hours • Cooker capacity 5 litres

1 kg (2 lb 3 oz) chicken breast fillets, diced
2 tablespoons plain (all-purpose) flour
1 tablespoon oil
⅓ cup soy sauce
¼ cup pineapple juice
3 tablespoons honey
2 tablespoons hoisin sauce
1 tablespoon apple cider vinegar
1½ teaspoon minced garlic
1 teaspoon minced ginger
2 tablespoons cornflour (cornstarch), mixed to a slurry with 2 tablespoons water

1. Place the chicken in a plastic bag with the flour and shake well to coat.

2. Heat the oil in the searing insert of a slow cooker or a frying pan over medium–high heat. Add the chicken and fry for about 5 minutes, until browned. Transfer to the slow cooker.

3. Combine all the remaining ingredients except the cornflour slurry in a bowl with ¼ cup of water, then pour into the slow cooker.

4. Cover and cook on high for 3 hours.

5. Stir in the cornflour slurry. Continue cooking for 5–10 minutes until the sauce is lovely and thick.

Chicken Fricassee

A classic dish with a slow-cooked twist. My family loves the creamy mushroom sauce. Serve this on brown rice or creamy mashed potato, with steamed vegetables.

Serves 4 • Preparation 15 mins • Cook 4–5 hours • Cooker capacity 6 litres

1 kg (2 lb 3 oz) skinless chicken thigh fillets
2 tablespoons plain (all-purpose) flour
1 tablespoon butter
1 onion, chopped
250 g (9 oz) button mushrooms, cut into quarters
2 garlic cloves, minced
¼ teaspoon dried thyme
¼ teaspoon dried tarragon
½ cup chicken stock
½ cup white wine
1 tablespoon cornflour (cornstarch), mixed to a slurry with 1 tablespoon water
150 ml (5 fl oz) cooking cream

1. Place the chicken in a plastic bag with the flour and shake well to coat.

2. Heat the butter in the searing insert of a slow cooker or a frying pan over medium–high heat. Add the chicken and fry until browned. Transfer to the slow cooker.

3. Add the onion, mushroom, garlic, thyme and tarragon and season with salt and pepper. Combine the stock and wine, then pour into the slow cooker.

4. Cover and cook on low for 4–5 hours.

5. Remove the chicken with a slotted spoon and set aside to keep warm.

6. Return the searing insert to the stovetop (or transfer the sauce to a saucepan). Stir in the cornflour slurry. Add the cream and cook over medium heat for about 5 minutes until the sauce is nice and thick.

7. Serve the chicken with the sauce poured over the top.

Creamy Mexican Chicken

A slow-cooked creamy Mexican shredded chicken dish the whole family can enjoy! If your children prefer chicken fillets to bone-in pieces, you can use those instead. This recipe is amazing served with fresh steamed green vegetables, rice, or even pasta.

Serves 5 • Preparation 15 mins • Cook 4½ hours • Cooker capacity 6 litres

5 chicken Maryland pieces (about 1.5 kg (3 lb 5 oz))
250 g (9 oz) block cream cheese, cubed
35 g (1 oz) packet taco seasoning mix
1 tablespoon cornflour (cornstarch)
150 ml (5 fl oz) cooking cream

1. Place the chicken in the slow cooker. Toss the cream cheese over the chicken and sprinkle the taco seasoning mix over the top.

2. Cover and cook on low for 4 hours.

3. Carefully lift out the chicken pieces, pull the meat from the bones and set aside (discard bones).

4. Give the sauce a really good whisk while the chicken is out, to break down any remaining cream cheese lumps. Mix the cornflour into the cream until smooth, then whisk into the sauce. Return the chicken to the cooker, cover and cook for a further 30 minutes.

⊨— Honey Balsamic Chicken —●

I use thigh cutlets for this recipe, but more budget-friendly cuts such as wings or drumsticks would be just as good. Don't be afraid to use whatever suits your family best. We like to serve this chicken with salads in summer, or with vegetables in the cooler months.

Serves 5 • Preparation 10 mins • Cook 5 hours • Cooker capacity 6 litres

1.5 kg (3 lb 5 oz) chicken pieces
½ cup balsamic vinegar
½ cup honey
½ cup brown sugar, firmly packed
¼ cup soy sauce
2 teaspoons minced garlic
1 teaspoon minced ginger

1. Place the chicken in the slow cooker. Combine all the other ingredients and pour over the chicken.

2. Cover and cook on low for 5 hours.

Barbecue Plum Chicken

This recipe was inspired by a sauce I created for the Asian Meatballs recipe from Slow Cooker Central book 1 – I absolutely love it! Because I eat a lot of chicken, I decided to try it with those same flavours, and I wasn't disappointed. We like to serve this with creamy mashed potato and vegetables so we can drizzle the sauce over the mash.

Serves 5 • Preparation 5 mins • Cook 5 hours • Cooker capacity 6 litres

10 chicken drumsticks
½ cup barbecue sauce
¼ cup plum sauce
2 tablespoons hoisin sauce
2 garlic cloves, minced
1 tablespoon cornflour (cornstarch), mixed to a slurry with 1 tablespoon water
Mashed potato and steamed vegetables, to serve

1. Place the chicken in the slow cooker. Combine all the other ingredients and pour over the chicken.

2. Cover and cook on low for 4 hours 50 minutes.

3. Stir in the cornflour slurry and cook for 10 minutes or until the sauce is thickened.

4. Serve with mashed potato and steamed vegetables.

Cheesy Salami Chicken

What's not to love about these three ingredients, especially when they're together! Jarlsberg is a lovely melting cheese that's perfect for this dish, but mozzarella would work too. We keep the salami mild for our children's tastebuds, but if you like heat, by all means use a hot salami. Our children love this recipe and ask for it often.

Serves 5 • Preparation 5 mins • Cook 4 hours • Cooker capacity 5 litres

5 chicken thigh cutlets (bone in), or chicken pieces of your choice
5 slices mild salami
5 slices Jarlsberg cheese

1. Place the chicken cutlets in the slow cooker. Cover and cook on high for 3 hours.

2. Carefully remove the chicken with a slotted spoon and set aside. Drain all the liquid from the slow cooker, then return the chicken.

3. Lay one slice of salami on top of each chicken piece, then place a slice of Jarlsberg on top (if you have excess cheese you can double it over).

4. Cover, putting a tea towel (dish towel) under the lid, and cook on low for 1 hour.

NOTE: You can adapt the quantities to make however many serves you need.

Creamy Garlic Chicken
Made Easy

An easy yet tasty, low-carb, cheesy, creamy chicken delight! This is delicious served with low-carb cauliflower 'rice' and steamed vegetables. Alternatively, if you aren't watching carbs, pair it with whipped potato mash.

Serves 3 • Preparation 15 mins • Cook 2 hours • Cooker capacity 5 litres

Vegetable oil
700 g (1 lb 9 oz) chicken thigh fillets, diced into small pieces
1 tablespoon minced garlic
300 ml (10 fl oz) cooking cream
1 cup grated tasty cheese, plus extra to serve

1. Heat a little oil in a searing slow cooker or on the stovetop. Add the chicken and garlic and cook until lightly browned.

2. Combine the chicken, garlic and cream in the slow cooker. Season with salt and pepper.

3. Cover, putting a tea towel (dish towel) under the lid, and cook on low for 2 hours.

4. Add the cheese and stir to melt. Serve with extra cheese sprinkled on top.

NOTE: Larger chicken pieces will require extra cooking time. The cooking cream is important as it resists splitting like normal cream.

Mustard Maple Chicken

A fabulous flavour combination that develops beautifully during slow cooking. The garlic adds a lovely depth, too.

Serves 4 • Preparation 5 Mins • Cook 4 hours • Cooker capacity 5 litres

1 kg (2 lb 4 oz) chicken thigh fillets
125 g (4½ oz/½ cup) Dijon mustard
3 tablespoons maple syrup
1 garlic clove, minced
Steamed broccolini, julienne carrots and baby potatoes, to serve

1. Place the chicken in the slow cooker.

2. Combine the remaining ingredients in a small bowl, pour over the chicken and toss to coat the chicken well in the mixture.

3. Cover and cook on low for 4 hours.

4. Serve with steamed broccolini, julienne carrots and baby potatoes.

French Cream Chicken with Four Ingredients

I created this ahhhh-mazing-tasting creamy chicken dish when I wanted something that would suit my low-carb life at the time but that the whole family could enjoy with me. It's also a great way to get your kids to eat more spinach for its exceptionally high nutritional value without them really noticing. Since I first cooked this recipe it has become a regular in our house – we love it that much.

Serves 2 • Preparation 15 mins • Cook 1 hour 20 mins • Cooker capacity 6 litres

Vegetable oil
500 g (1 lb 2 oz) chicken thigh fillets, diced
110 g (3¾ oz) block French onion cream cheese (see note), diced
200 ml (6½ fl oz) cooking cream
60 g (2 oz) baby spinach leaves

1. Heat a little oil in a searing slow cooker or frying pan. Brown the chicken then transfer to the slow cooker. Add the cream cheese and stir for 2–3 minutes to melt and coat the chicken. Stir in the cooking cream.

2. Cover, putting a tea towel (dish towel) under the lid, and cook on high for 1¼ hours

3. Add the spinach, stir until wilted, then serve.

NOTES: If you can't source French onion flavoured cream cheese, you could use regular cream cheese and add 20 g (¾ oz) of dry French onion soup mix. Or you could vary the flavour by using another variety of cream cheese: sweet chilli, chive and onion, or apricot.

Replacing the baby spinach with semidried tomatoes is another yummy option.

The cooking cream is important because it resists splitting like normal cream.

This recipe can be doubled to feed a larger crowd. This won't affect the cooking time much; about 15 minutes extra will be all that's needed.

Poached Chicken Breast

I first made this because I wanted chopped chicken on hand for sandwiches and school lunches. Ready-cooked chicken meat is expensive and I didn't like using a whole chicken because that meant removing the skin and the bones. This recipe produces moist, tender 100% chicken breast. You can easily vary the flavour with additional herbs and spices – I kept this one generic for use in other dishes and sandwiches, but see the notes below for a version with Asian flavours.

Serves 8 • Preparation 5 mins • Cook 2 hours • Cooker capacity 5 litres

4 chicken breast fillets
Pinch of garlic salt
Pinch of onion powder
1 teaspoon chicken stock powder
1 cup hot water

1. Put the chicken breasts in the slow cooker. Sprinkle with the garlic salt, onion powder and stock. Season with pepper and pour in the hot water.

2. Cover and cook on high for 2 hours.

3. Remove and dice or shred chicken to desired size.

NOTES: To make poached chicken with Asian flavours, use the same quantity of chicken breasts and the same cooking time, but replace the other ingredients with 2 cups chicken stock, 1 tablespoon soy sauce, 2 teaspoons minced garlic, 2 teaspoons sesame oil and 1 heaped teaspoon minced ginger.

The chicken can be frozen in bags in small serves, perfect for sandwiches, wraps and other dishes requiring cooked chicken.

Creamy Chicken Cup-a-Laksa

This is a quick, easy kind of recipe with simple ingredients – a huge success with our kids too. You could swap out drumsticks for any chicken cut or fillet you prefer. This dish has a mild laksa flavour, not spicy, so it's very suitable for the whole family.

Serves 5 • Preparation 5 mins • Cook 5 hours • Cooker capacity 6 litres

10 chicken drumsticks
300 ml (10 fl oz) cooking cream
65 g (2 oz) (2 sachets) Asian laksa soup mix (no water added)
Brown rice or cauliflower mash and steamed green vegetables, to serve

1. Place the chicken in the slow cooker. Combine the cream and soup mix and pour over the chicken.
2. Cover and cook on low for 5 hours.
3. Serve with brown rice or cauliflower mash and green veggies.

NOTE: You could shred the chicken, remove the bones and stir the meat through the sauce if you prefer.

Sweet Soy Asian Chicken

These delicious chicken pieces have a sweet Asian flavour. If you love Chinese food like I do, you'll love this. You could replace the thigh cutlets with any other cut of chicken, or use fillets.

Serves 4 • Preparation 10 mins • Cook 4½ hours • Cooker capacity 6 litres

8 chicken thigh cutlets (bone in, skin on)
½ cup kecap manis (sweet soy sauce)
2 tablespoons sweet chilli sauce
1 tablespoon minced garlic
1 tablespoon minced ginger
Brown rice and Asian greens, to serve

1. Place the chicken in the slow cooker. Combine the other ingredients and pour over the chicken.

2. Cover and cook on low for 4½ hours. If you are around, baste the chicken with sauce occasionally during the cooking time, for a rich final colour.

3. Serve with brown rice and Asian greens.

Honey and Garlic Chicken

The flavours in this dish are so yummy and you can use whichever cut of chicken you like. I find drumsticks and thigh fillets are much juicier than breast when cooked this way. Serve it with rice and vegetables.

Serves 4 • Preparation 5 mins • Cook 4–6 hours • Cooker capacity 5 litres

1 kg (2 lb 4 oz) chicken thigh fillets or drumsticks
½ cup tomato sauce (ketchup)
½ cup honey
⅓ cup soy sauce
3 garlic cloves, minced
Brown rice and Asian greens, to serve

1. Put the chicken in the slow cooker. Combine the tomato sauce, honey, soy sauce and garlic in a small bowl and pour the mixture over the chicken.

2. Cover and cook on low for 4–6 hours.

3. Remove the meat from the drumsticks (if using drumsticks), discard the bones and return the meat to the sauce. Serve with brown rice and Asian greens.

Naked Chicken Parmigiana

Super easy, super tasty – it's naked parmigiana! It's just like regular parmi but without the crumbs, and still with all the cheesy tomato goodness you expect. Serve this with chips and salad or veggies.

Serves 4 • Preparation 10 mins • Cook 4¼ hours • Cooker capacity 6 litres

1 kg (2 lb 3 oz) chicken thigh fillets
500 g (1 lb 2 oz) bottle napoletana or parmigiana sauce (see note)
200 g (7 oz) grated mozzarella cheese

1. Place the chicken in the slow cooker and pour the sauce over.

2. Cover and cook on low for 4 hours.

3. Sprinkle the chicken with cheese. Cover, putting a tea towel (dish towel) under the lid, and cook for a further 15 minutes or until the cheese has melted.

NOTE: Use your favourite sauce – I used chunky tomato with herbs.

You can remove some of the excess cooking liquid, if you like, by scooping it out with a large spoon, before you add the cheese.

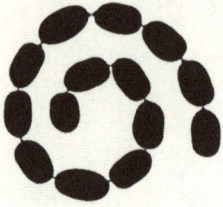

SAUSAGES

Sweet Sauce Sausages

I love a good slow-cooked sausage recipe. Not only are sausages budget friendly, but they're easy to prepare and cook, and the kids love sausages for dinner – they always eat it with minimal complaints. This dish has so few ingredients that the kids could even get involved in helping you to cook it!

Serves 6 • Preparation 10 mins • Cook 4–5 hours • Cooker capacity 5 litres

12 thin sausages
¾ cup apricot jam (jelly)
¾ cup BBQ sauce
1 tablespoon cornflour (cornstarch), mixed to a slurry with 1 tablespoon water (optional)

1. Place the sausages in the slow cooker. Combine all the other ingredients with ½ cup of water and pour the mixture over the sausages.
2. Cover and cook on low for 4½ hours.
3. Check the consistency of the sauce, and if you'd like it thicker, add the cornflour slurry and cook for another 30 minutes.

NOTES: You can use cornflour to thicken the sauce, as described, or you could use the tea towel trick: for the last 2 hours of cooking, place a tea towel (dish towel) under the lid. This will absorb some of the condensation and you'll end up with a slightly thicker sauce.

In the last hour or so of cooking time, I use a plastic egg flip or spoon to 'cut' the sausages into bite-sized pieces in the pot. By this time they're very tender and it's easy to do.

Sweet Chilli Sausages

If you love sweet chilli, you'll love this recipe – it's a great budget-friendly twist on a classic taste. I use beef sausages, but chicken or pork sausages would also work. Mild enough for the whole family to enjoy.

Serves 6 • Preparation 15 mins • Cook 5 hours • Cooker capacity 5 litres

12 thin beef sausages (or any other sausages)
1½ cups beef stock
1 green capsicum (pepper), sliced
1 small red onion, sliced
¾ cup sweet chilli sauce
Rice and steamed broccoli, to serve

1. Combine all the ingredients in the slow cooker. Cover and cook on low for 5 hours.
2. Serve with rice and steamed broccoli.

Roast Vegetable, Sausage & Gravy One Pot Dinner

As a time-poor mum to a big family, there's nothing I love more than a one pot dinner. Less time in the kitchen and less washing up is a win-win. My children love sausages, so this was a hit with them. This recipe combines roast veg and gravy with sausages all ready to serve for a complete meal.

Serves 5 • Preparation 20 mins • Cook 5 hours • Cooker capacity 7 litres

5 large pumpkin (squash) chunks (I leave the skin on)
5 large sweet potato chunks
5 baby potatoes
5 baby carrots (or use large carrots cut in two)
10 thin beef sausages, cut in half
3 cups cold gravy (see note)

1. Arrange the vegetables in the slow cooker and top with the sausages. Pour the gravy over.
2. Cover and cook on high for 5 hours or until the vegetables are perfectly tender but not mushy.
3. To serve, divide the sausages and vegetables between plates and pour the gravy over.

NOTE: To make gravy, use a gravy powder mix and follow the packet directions to make 3 cups, but use cold water instead of hot.

Devilled Sausages

Back in the days before I owned a slow cooker, one of my favourite packet meal bases was devilled sausages. Now I'll never need to buy the packet version again, because I can create it from scratch so easily! Our children love this served with mashed potato and steamed vegetables.

Serves 6 • Preparation 15 mins • Cook 5–6 hours • Cooker capacity 5 litres

1 large brown onion, sliced
12 thin beef sausages
1 large green apple, skin on, cored and sliced
80 g (3 oz) tomato paste (concentrated purée)
2 tablespoons Worcestershire sauce
1 tablespoon brown sugar
1 teaspoon mustard powder
½ teaspoon curry powder
Mashed potato and steamed vegetables, to serve

1. Spread the onion in the base of the slow cooker. Arrange the sausages on top, then add the apple.

2. Combine all the other ingredients with 1½ cups water and pour the mixture over the sausages.

3. Cover and cook on low for 5–6 hours.

4. Serve with mashed potato and steamed vegetables.

NOTES: If your slow cooker runs hot, you might need to add an extra ½ cup water during cooking.

If you'd like a thicker sauce, stir in 1 tablespoon cornflour (cornstarch) mixed to a slurry with 1 tablespoon water about 15–20 minutes before the end of the cooking time.

Chicken Stroganoff Sausages

I love taking a classic recipe and giving it a twist. When most people think of stroganoff, they think of beef. But why not chicken, and why not sausages? I tried it, and the result was even better than I'd expected! It's almost impossible to go wrong with slow-cooked sausages, and they're better on the budget than beef. This is great served with pasta, rice or creamy mashed potato and vegetables.

Serves 4 • Preparation 15 mins • Cook 4 hours 15mins • Cooker capacity 3.5 litres

8 thin chicken sausages
6–8 large flat mushrooms, thinly sliced
1 large onion, thinly sliced
1 tablespoon chicken stock powder dissolved in 1 cup warm water
2 tablespoons Worcestershire sauce
2 teaspoons minced garlic
1½ teaspoons sweet paprika
200 ml (6½ fl oz) sour cream mixed with 1 tablespoon cornflour

1. Place the sausages in the slow cooker and top with the mushroom and onion.
2. Combine stock, Worcestershire sauce, garlic and paprika and pour the mixture over the sausages.
3. Cover and cook on low for 4 hours.
4. Remove the sausages, cut them into slices and return them to the pot. Or leave them whole if you prefer – I like to cut mine.
5. Add the sour cream mixture and stir to combine.
6. Cook for 10–15 minutes or until the sauce has thickened.

Mushroom Sausages

Add four ingredients to the slow cooker, turn it on and walk away. Does it get any easier? This is delicious served with rice and vegetables.

Serves 6 • Preparation 10 mins • Cook 5–6 hours • Cooker capacity 6 litres

12 thin beef sausages
2 x 440 g (15½ oz) cans condensed cream of mushroom soup
2 brown onions, sliced
2 cups sliced button mushrooms

1. Place the sausages in the slow cooker. Pour the soup over (don't add any water). Add the onion and mushroom and stir to combine.

2. Cover and cook on low 5–6 hours.

NOTE: In the last hour or so of cooking time, I use a plastic egg flip or spoon to 'cut' the sausages into bite-sized pieces in the pot. By this time they're very tender and it's easy to do.

Chutney & Tomato Sausages

These sweet, fruity, tomato sauce sausages go perfectly with creamy mashed potato and assorted veg. This is a meal the whole family can enjoy.

Serves 6 • Preparation 15 mins • Cook 6 hours • Cooker capacity 6 litres

12 thin beef sausages
1 large onion, diced
400 g (14 oz) can diced tomatoes
250 g (9 oz) jar fruit chutney
2 teaspoons dried parsley flakes
Mashed potato and steamed vegetables, to serve

1. Place the sausages in the slow cooker and add the onion.
2. Combine the tomatoes, chutney and parsley and pour the mixture over the sausages.
3. Cover and cook on low for 6 hours.
4. Serve with mashed potato and steamed vegetables.

Mango Coconut Curry Sausages

This recipe combines several of my favourite things. Mango is my most favourite fruit in the world, I love a good curry, and I love making sausages for the family because I know the kids will always eat them without complaint. So this dish is a win-win-win! Adjust the amount of curry powder to suit your family's tastes and serve this with rice or mash and veg.

Serves 6 • Preparation 20 mins • Cook 6 hours • Cooker capacity 6 litres

12 thin sausages
1 onion, diced
425 g (15 oz) can mango pieces in syrup
400 ml (13½ fl oz) can coconut milk
1 tablespoon minced garlic
1 tablespoon curry powder
1 tablespoon cornflour (cornstarch)
1 cup sliced spring onions (scallions)

1. Place the sausages and onion in the slow cooker.
2. Blend the mango and syrup to a pulp using a blender or stick blender. Add all the remaining ingredients except the spring onion and blitz to combine well. Pour the mixture over the sausages.
3. Cover and cook on low for 5½ hours.
4. Add the spring onion and cook for 30 minutes.

NOTES: The heat factor in this curry is medium. You could halve the amount of curry powder to reduce it to mild. I use Keen's brand curry powder.

Another way to reduce the heat for kids is to mix half a cup of pouring cream through theirs before serving it. Our children enjoyed this dish with brown rice, and the adults liked it with mashed sweet potato.

In the last hour or so of cooking time, I use a plastic egg flip or spoon to 'cut' the sausages into bite-sized pieces in the pot. By this time they're very tender and it's easy to do.

Sausages in Barbecue & Mustard Sauce

Slice these sausages into bite-size pieces and serve them on toothpicks at your next party. Or just leave them whole and enjoy them with salad or steamed vegies.

Serves 6 • Preparation 5 Mins • Cook 4 hours • Cooker capacity 6 litres

1 kg (2 lb 3 oz) thin beef sausages
½ cup barbecue sauce
½ cup light brown sugar
2 tablespoons mild American mustard
1 tablespoon white vinegar
1 tablespoon soy sauce
1 garlic clove, minced
Salad or steamed vegies, to serve

1. Put the sausages in the slow cooker (pre-browning is optional but not required). Combine the remaining ingredients and pour the mixture over the sausages.

2. Cover and cook on low for 4 hours.

3. Slice or serve whole with salad or steamed vegetables.

NOTE: You can leave the sausages in the slow cooker on the warm setting for another couple of hours if you need to – for a party, for example.

Curried Sausages

Who doesn't love a good curry made in the slow cooker? This version doesn't have the cream base of some, and it can be made with low-fat sausages so it's friendly on the waistline. Load it up with vegetables for maximum goodness.

Serves 4 • Preparation 10 mins • Cook 6–8 hours • Cooker capacity 5 litres

500 g (1 lb 2 oz) thick or thin sausages
1 large onion, diced
4 potatoes, cubed
3 carrots, coarsely chopped
1 cup frozen peas
1–2 tablespoons curry powder, to taste
3 cups beef stock
1–2 tablespoon cornflour (cornstarch), mixed to a slurry with 1–2 tablespoons
    water
Steamed rice, to serve

1. Put the sausages in the slow cooker. (I put mine in raw but you can boil them first and remove the skins if you prefer.) Add the remaining ingredients, cover and cook on low for 6–8 hours.

2. Remove the sausages from the sauce, slice them and set them aside.

3. Check whether the sauce needs thickening. If it does, stir in the cornflour slurry.

4. Return the sausages to the sauce and cook for 10 minutes, until the sausages are heated through and the sauce has thickened if required.

5. Serve the curried sausages with rice.

Creamy Satay Sausages

I created this dish because I noticed a gap in the satay recipes I'd seen. Satay beef, satay chicken, satay everything except satay sausages! So I decided to make them myself and they turned out great. The same recipe can, of course, be used for other meats if you prefer. It's a thick, almost fluffy (for lack of a better word) satay sauce that isn't spicy – suitable for children and adults alike. Note the recipe uses cooking cream, which is less prone to splitting than regular cream.

Serves 6 • Preparation 5 mins • Cook 4–5 hours • Cooker capacity 5 litres

12 thin beef sausages, cut into thirds
300 ml (10 fl oz) reduced-fat cooking cream
1 cup peanut butter (smooth or crunchy)
1 teaspoon curry powder
2 tablespoons sweet chilli sauce

1. Put the sausages in the slow cooker. Combine the remaining ingredients in a bowl with 1 cup water, then pour into the slow cooker.
2. Cover and cook on low for 4–5 hours.

NOTE: You can brown or pre-cook the sausages before adding them to the slow cooker, but I don't find it necessary.

If your slow cooker runs 'hot', you might need to add an extra 1–2 cups water during cooking so you get a saucy finish. Just check as you go along, and if it's drying out, add water.

Sweet Sausage Curry

Sausages are such a versatile option when you're on a budget. Many recipes that use other meats can be made with sausages instead, and a curry is no different. This serves our family of five with leftovers for at least another two serves, and it's great to fill hungry tummies at the end of a long day. Serve it with creamy mashed potato for a filling meal that won't break the bank.

Serves 8 • Preparation 15 mins • Cook 5 hours • Cooker capacity 6 litres

16 thin beef sausages
2 onions, diced
2 small Granny Smith apples, peeled, cored and diced
1½ cups beef stock
⅔ cup fruit chutney
3 teaspoons mild curry powder
2 garlic cloves, minced
½ teaspoon minced ginger
Mashed potato and steamed vegetables, to serve

1. Cut the sausages into chunks (about 6 pieces per sausage). Place the sausages, onion and apple in the slow cooker.

2. Combine the other ingredients and pour the mixture into the slow cooker.

3. Cover and cook on low for 5 hours.

4. Serve with mashed potato and vegetables.

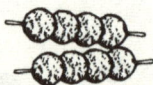

BEEF

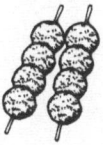

Bacon and Barbecue Brisket

Brisket is a classic budget-friendly choice for slow cooking. Combining it with bacon and a delicious sauce produces a really versatile pulled meat that's equally tasty paired with vegetable mash, hot chips or even just bread rolls.

Serves 6-8 • Preparation 15 mins • Cook 8 hours • Cooker capacity 6 litres

1.5 kg piece beef brisket (see note)
400 g (14 oz) can condensed cream of mushroom soup
200 g (7 oz) diced bacon
1 large onion, diced
½ cup barbecue sauce
2 teaspoons beef stock powder
2 garlic cloves
1 tablespoon cornflour (cornstarch), mixed to a slurry with 1 tablespoon water (optional)

1. Combine all the ingredients in the slow cooker. Cover and cook on high for 8 hours.

2. Pull the brisket into shreds. You can do this in the slow cooker using plastic non-scratch utensils, or on a cutting board. The long, slow cooking means the meat can be pulled apart very easily.

3. Return the meat to the slow cooker and stir to coat it in the sauce. It will absorb a lot of the liquid.

4. Check the consistency of the sauce, and if you'd like it thicker (if you're using the meat as a pie filling, for example), add the cornflour slurry and cook for another 10 minutes.

NOTE: You want regular brisket for this recipe, not corned silverside brisket.

Beef Hot Pot

This is a great meal to take camping! I cook it at home and freeze it, transport it in the esky, then defrost it and heat it over the campfire for an easy dinner for hungry little campers. It's equally good at home on a cold night, served with crusty bread rolls for dunking in the sauce.

Serves 5 • Preparation 20 mins • Cook 7–8 hours • Cooker capacity 6 litres

1 kg casserole beef, diced (eg gravy beef, chuck steak)
2 large onions, diced
425 g (15 oz) can condensed tomato soup
6–8 baby potatoes, skin on, quartered
4 small carrots, sliced
1 tablespoon Dijon mustard
2 teaspoons minced garlic
2 teaspoons cracked black pepper

1. Place all the ingredients in the slow cooker and stir to combine.

2. Cover and cook on high for 7–8 hours.

3. Serve with crusty bread rolls for a hearty one-pot dinner.

▬ Saucy Shredded Brisket ➤

Brisket is made for slow cooking! The long and slow process makes it melt-in-your-mouth tender, and this recipe is no exception. When you shred the meat, it will soak up all the liquid and you'll have saucy shredded beef ready to go with your favourite veg or on sliders with slaw.

Serves 6–8 • Preparation 15 mins • Cook 6–8 hours • Cooker capacity 6 litres

1–2 kg (2 lb 3 oz–4 lb 6 oz) piece beef brisket (see note)
1 large onion, sliced
1 cup tomato sauce (ketchup)
¼ cup mild mustard
¼ cup brown sugar
1 teaspoon smoked paprika

1. Place the brisket in the slow cooker and top with the onion. Combine all the other ingredients and pour the mixture over the brisket.

2. Cover and cook on high for 6–8 hours (depending on the size of the brisket), until the meat is pull-apart tender.

3. Pull the brisket into shreds. You can do this in the slow cooker using plastic non-scratch utensils, or on a cutting board.

4. Return the meat to the slow cooker and stir to coat it in the sauce. It will absorb a lot of the liquid.

NOTE: You want regular brisket for this recipe, not corned silverside brisket.

Hungarian Beef Goulash

In years gone by, long before I started slow cooking, I used to make goulash using a meal base from a packet. Somewhere along the way, I just stopped making it. But then I remembered it by chance, and it was only natural that I wanted to try making my own version in the slow cooker. This is mild enough for the whole family to enjoy and goes really nicely with creamy mashed potato.

Serves 5 • Preparation 20 mins • Cook 6–8 hours • Cooker capacity 6 litres

1–1.5 kg (2 lb 3 oz–4 lb 6 oz) casserole beef, diced (eg chuck steak, oyster blade)
2 cups beef stock
400 g (14 oz) can diced tomato
1 large onion, sliced
1 large red capsicum (pepper), sliced
2 tablespoons tomato paste (concentrated purée)
2 tablespoons paprika
½ teaspoon salt
½ teaspoon cracked black pepper
2 tablespoons cornflour (cornstarch), mixed to a slurry with 2 tablespoons water (optional)

1. Combine all the ingredients except the cornflour slurry in the slow cooker.
2. Cover and cook on auto for 5½ hours (2 hours on high, then 3½ hours on low), or on low for 7½ hours.
3. Check the consistency of the sauce. If you'd like it thicker, stir in the cornflour slurry.
4. Cook for another 30 minutes.
5. Serve with creamy mashed potato

NOTE: If you like a very creamy sauce, stir in 1 cup sour cream just before serving. We like it best without.

Complete Roast Beef Dinner

There's nothing quite like a roast done in the slow cooker. However, you don't want to have to heat up the oven just for the vegetables. With this recipe, you don't need to. EVERYTHING is cooked in the slow cooker: tender roast beef and an array of vegetables to fill your plate. Just add gravy and dinner is done. Sunday roast sorted!

Serves 5 • Preparation 15 mins • Cook 8 hours • Cooker capacity 6 litres

2 kg (4 lb 6 oz) beef blade roast (I used 2 x 1 kg (2 lb 3 oz) pieces)
Seasoning of your choice (I like paprika, onion, salt, garlic salt, and pepper; see note)
1 teaspoon olive oil
100 ml (3½ fl oz) red wine (eg shiraz; see note)
5 or more baby potatoes, skin on
1 sweet potato, cut into 3
3 large carrots, halved
1 jap pumpkin wedge, skin on, cut into 3 (see note)
1 large brown onion, whole
5–10 Brussels sprouts
1 bunch asparagus, woody ends removed
Gravy, to serve (see note)

1. Season the beef generously with the seasoning blend of your choice.

2. Heat the oil in the searing insert of a slow cooker or a frying pan over medium–high heat. Add the beef and sear for about 5 minutes on each side, until browned. Transfer the beef (or the searing insert) to the slow cooker.

3. Pour the wine over the beef, then arrange the potato, sweet potato and carrot around the beef. Cover and cook on low for 2 hours.

4. Add the pumpkin and onion and cook for another 5 hours.

5. Arrange the Brussels sprouts around the beef, and the asparagus on top of the beef. Cook for another 1 hour.

6. Check that the vegetables are tender. You'll notice that the meat has released a lot of liquid.

7. Remove the beef and allow it to rest for a few minutes. Meanwhile, gently transfer the vegetables to serving plates.

8. Carve the beef and serve with gravy.

NOTES: The blend of spices I've suggested can be purchased as ready-made 'steak seasoning'.

Replace the wine with stock if you prefer. However, the wine doesn't leave a strong taste in the meat or vegetables.

I like to leave the skin on the pumpkin because it helps to hold it together. You could remove the skin during serving.

I cut the vegetables into large pieces to cook them, and leave the onion whole, but on serving you can cut them into smaller pieces to suit the number of people you need to feed. You can use whatever vegetables you like.

Browning the beef before slow-cooking is optional.

For gravy, you could thicken the cooking juices with instant gravy powder if you like.

■— 'Roast' Beef —●

Herbs and spices give the cooking liquid here an amazing flavour. I like to drizzle a few spoons of it over the finished roast for a delicious sauce, but you could serve traditional gravy if you prefer. This is great accompanied by roast vegetables or served on bread rolls.

Serves 4 • Preparation 10 Mins • Cook 6 hours • Cooker capacity 5 litres

Oil spray, for frying
1 kg (2 lb 3 oz) beef roast
½ cup beef stock
1 tablespoon wholegrain mustard
1 tablespoon tomato paste (concentrated purée)
1 tablespoon Worcestershire sauce
2 garlic cloves, minced
1 teaspoon fresh thyme leaves
1 teaspoon fresh rosemary leaves
1 teaspoon cracked black pepper
Roast vegetables, to serve

1. Spray the searing insert of a slow cooker or a frying pan with oil, and heat over medium–high heat. Add the beef and sear for about 5 minutes on each side, until browned. Transfer the beef (or the searing insert) to the slow cooker.

2. Combine all the other ingredients and pour the mixture over the beef. Cover and cook on low for 6 hours, basting every now and then, and turning the meat once during cooking.

3. Slice the roast and drizzle with a little of the juices. Serve with your favourite roast vegetables.

Roast Beef with Rich Gravy

Make your next roast dinner easy and tasty with this great recipe! Tender roast beef, slow cooked in and served with a rich roast meat gravy – yum! Serve with your favourite assorted roast vegetables or on bread rolls

Serves 6 • Preparation 15 mins • Cook 6–8 hours • Cooker capacity 6 litres

2 kg (4 lb 6 oz) piece beef blade or topside roast
1 large onion, quartered
1½ tablespoons American mustard
27 g (1 oz) sachet instant roast meat gravy powder

SPICE RUB
1½ teaspoons smoked paprika
¾ teaspoon garlic powder
½ teaspoon pink Himalayan salt
½ teaspoon cracked black pepper
¼ teaspoon ground cumin

1. Place the beef in the slow cooker and pierce holes all over the top with the tip of a sharp knife. Arrange the onion around the beef, and spread the mustard over the top.

2. To make the spice rub, combine the ingredients in a small bowl. Rub onto and into the beef.

3. Cover and cook on high for 4 hours, then on low for 2 hours. (Alternatively, cook on auto for 7 hours, or on low for 8 hours.)

4. Carefully lift the beef from the cooker and place on a board or platter. Cover with foil and set aside to rest. Remove the onion using a slotted spoon and discard it.

5. Add the gravy powder to the cooking juices in the slow cooker and whisk to combine well. Cover and cook on high for 10–15 minutes, until thickened.

6. Carve the beef and serve with gravy.

➤— Beef and Red Wine Casserole —➤

This traditional slow cooker recipe is very popular. Adjust the vegetables to suit yourself – it's a great way to use up all your leftover vegetables before shopping day. With crusty bread rolls on the side, this makes a complete meal.

Serves 4–6 • Preparation 10 Mins • Cook 3–4 or 6–8 hours • Cooker capacity 6 litres

¼ cup plain (all-purpose) flour
Salt and cracked black pepper, to taste
1.5 kg (3 lb 5 oz) blade steak, cubed
2 tablespoons vegetable oil
1 brown onion, sliced
4 garlic cloves, minced
½ cup tomato paste (concentrated purée)
½ cup red wine
2 tablespoons beef stock powder
400 g (14 oz) can diced tomatoes
2 cups sliced mushrooms
1 tablespoon oregano leaves
Steamed baby potatoes and green beans, to serve
Crusty bread rolls, to serve

1. Combine the flour, salt and pepper in a bowl, add the steak and toss to coat.

2. Heat the oil in a frying pan over high heat, then brown the meat in batches, stirring often. Transfer the meat to the slow cooker.

3. Add the onion and garlic to the pan and cook for 2 minutes, stirring, until beginning to brown. Add the tomato paste, wine and stock powder and cook for 2 minutes, stirring constantly. Add the onion mixture to the slow cooker, then stir in the tomatoes, mushrooms and oregano.

4. Cover and cook for 3–4 hours on high or 6–8 hours on low.

5. Serve with steamed baby potatoes and green beans, with bread rolls on the side.

Beef Strips in Sweet Soy Sauce

An Asian-style stir-fry in your slow cooker? It can be done. I use an inexpensive cut of beef and still it comes out absolutely tender. Be sure to use sweet kecap manis soy sauce for this recipe, not regular soy sauce. Serve with brown rice and Asian vegetables.

Serves 4 • Preparation 15 mins • Cook 3 hours • Cooker capacity 5 litres

1 kg (2 lb 3 oz) gravy beef or chuck steak, sliced into strips
2–3 tablespoons plain (all-purpose) flour
1 tablespoon vegetable oil
1 onion, thinly sliced
1 cup hot water
½ cup kecap manis (sweet soy sauce)
2 beef stock cubes, crumbled
2 garlic cloves, minced
Sliced spring onions (scallions) and sesame seeds, to garnish

1. Place the beef in a plastic bag with the flour and shake well to coat.

2. Heat the oil in the searing insert of a slow cooker or a frying pan over medium–high heat. Add the beef and onion and stir-fry until browned. Transfer the beef and onion (or the searing insert) to the slow cooker.

3. Combine the water, kecap manis, stock cubes and garlic in a bowl, then pour the mixture over the beef.

4. Cover and cook on low for 3 hours, stirring once after 2 hours (if possible).

5. Serve garnished with spring onions and sesame seeds.

1-2-3 Roast Beef

This recipe was inspired by Grace Macdonald, a member of the Slow Cooker Central group on Facebook who made a similar recipe with pork – thanks Grace! I had beef to use up one day and easily adapted Grace's recipe. It was amazing! It's now become a regular in our house, and it's as easy as 1–2–3!

Serves 4 • Preparation 5 mins • Cook 6–8 hours • Cooker capacity 6 litres

1 kg (2 lb 3 oz) rolled rib beef roast (see note)
1½ tablespoons gravy powder (I use traditional)
½ cup warm water
Roast vegetables, to serve

1. Place the beef in the slow cooker and sprinkle with gravy powder. Pour the warm water over the beef.

2. Cover and cook on low for 6 hours, or longer if you are using a larger roast.

3. Slice and serve with the gravy and roast vegetables.

NOTE: You can use a larger piece of beef if you like.

Nanny's Braised Steak

This melt-in-your-mouth-tender steak in gravy will make you want to lick your plate! My mum used to make this on the stove for me when I was a child. We lost our mum when we were quite young, so this is a recipe I hold very dear as it always takes me back to that time. The grandchildren she never met now help me prepare and LOVE to eat 'Nanny's recipe', which makes me very proud. I know she would be bursting with pride to see her recipe in this book for everyone to enjoy. This one's for you, Mum. xx

Serves 4 • Preparation 15 mins • Cook 5 hours • Cooker capacity 6 litres

¼ cup mild American mustard
¼ cup brown sugar
1 kg (2 lb 3 oz) oyster blade steak (or any affordable casserole-style steak)
2 heaped tablespoons plain (all-purpose) flour
1 large onion, thinly sliced
½ cup tomato sauce (ketchup)
1½ tablespoons soy sauce
Mashed potato and vegetables, to serve

1. Combine the mustard and sugar in a freezer bag. Add the steak. Rub and shake the bag to coat the steaks with the mixture.

2. Place the flour in another freezer bag and season with salt and pepper. Tip the steak from the first bag into the second bag and toss to dust with flour.

3. Remove the steak from the bag and place in a single layer in the slow cooker. Top with the onion. Combine the tomato sauce and soy sauce and pour the mixture over the steak.

4. Cover and cook on low for 5 hours.

5. Serve with mashed potato and vegetables, with the gravy poured over.

NOTE: You don't need any water in this recipe, but you could add ½ cup for extra gravy if you like.

Family Friendly Beef Curry

Our family loves a good curry, but with children ranging in age from 16 down to 5, we need to keep the heat out of it so we can all enjoy the same meal. This curry based on coconut cream is very mild. You'll be sure to want seconds!

Serves 5 • Preparation 15 mins • Cook 7 hours • Cooker capacity 6 litres

1 kg (2 lb 3 oz) blade steak, cubed
1 large onion, diced
400 ml (13½ fl oz) can coconut cream
1 tablespoon minced garlic
1 tablespoon soy sauce
1 tablespoon brown sugar
3 teaspoons mild curry powder
2 teaspoons minced ginger
2 teaspoons cornflour (cornstarch)
½ teaspoon ground turmeric
1 tablespoon cornflour (cornstarch), mixed to a slurry with 1 tablespoon water

1. Place the beef and onion in the slow cooker. Combine all the other ingredients (except the cornflour slurry) and pour the mixture over the beef.

2. Cover and cook on low for 6½ hours.

3. Stir in the cornflour slurry and cook for another 30 minutes.

NOTE: If you like a hotter curry, add more curry powder. The cooking time will easily stretch to 8 hours if that works for you.

━ Sticky Steakhouse Ribs ━

Nothing says 'good ribs' like sticky little faces licking their fingers clean! Our kids love these ribs served with chunky chips and slaw for a fun weekend meal.

Serves 4–6 • Preparation 15 mins • Cook 6–8 hours • Cooker capacity 6 litres

1.5 kg beef spare ribs (the really meaty kind on wide flat bones)
1 onion, finely grated
⅔ cup steak sauce (your favourite)
2 tablespoons yellow mustard
2 tablespoons brown sugar
1 tablespoon minced garlic
1 teaspoon smoked paprika

1. Place the ribs in the slow cooker. Combine all the other ingredients to make the marinade. Reserve ½ cup marinade for later, and pour the remainder over the ribs.

2. Cook on auto for 6 hours or on low for 8 hours.

3. Carefully transfer the super-tender ribs to an oven tray and baste with the reserved marinade. Cook under a hot grill for about 10 minutes or until browned and glazed with the sticky sauce. Don't put the meat too close to the heat source, and take care that it doesn't burn.

⊨— Corned Beef —●

Slow-cooked corned beef is super-popular, and there are many, many versions of it. Here is a basic method that you can adapt to suit your taste. I've suggested some other flavourings below (see the notes), but you're limited only by your imagination.

Serves 4 • Preparation 5 mins • Cook 6–8 hours • Cooker capacity 6 litres

1 large onion, cut into quarters
2 garlic cloves, minced
1.5 kg (3 lb 5 oz) piece corned beef, rinsed (see note)
2 cups hot water
4 whole cloves
4 black peppercorns
2 fresh or dried bay leaves
Vegetables, to serve (see note)

1. Put the onion and garlic in the slow cooker, and put the beef on top.
2. Combine the hot water, cloves, peppercorns and bay leaves in a bowl and pour over the meat. Cover and cook on low for 6–8 hours.
3. Serve with vegetables of your choice.

NOTES: 'Corned beef' refers to beef that's been cured by the butcher in brine. In Australia, the cut of beef most often used to make corned beef is silverside, so the terms 'silverside' and 'corned beef' are used almost interchangeably.

For Lemonade Corned Beef or Ginger Beer Corned Beef, replace all ingredients other than the beef with a 1.25 litre (2½ pint) bottle of lemonade, ginger beer or ginger ale. The drink gives the meat a subtle flavour and the carbonation helps make it super-tender. You can also use sugar-free soft drink (soda) or even sparkling mineral water for a low-carb alternative.

For Citrus Corned Beef, replace all ingredients other than the beef with a 1.25 litre (2½ pint) bottle of sparkling mineral water, 1 lemon (halved) and 1 lime (halved).

It's easy to cook vegetables alongside the corned beef, and you can use whatever vegies you like. Place them in an oven bag. Tie the bag and pierce it at the top to allow venting. Submerge the bag carefully in the liquid in the slow cooker, leaving the pierced area and the tie out of the water. Timing depends on the vegetables you choose. Add hard vegetables, such as potato, carrot and sweet potato, 3 hours before the corned beef is done. Add soft vegetables, like zucchini, asparagus or broccoli, 1 hour before the corned beef is done. Check for tenderness before serving. You can add multiple bags if they fit.

FISH AND SEAFOOD

⊨— Curried Prawns —●

When I was a child, my dad made the BEST curried prawns, albeit on the stove. Recently I asked him how he did it, and I couldn't believe how simple it was to re-create in the slow cooker. The mild curry flavour is friendly for even small palates, but you can add extra curry powder if you like it spicy. I add a little saffron for a vivid yellow colour.

Serves 4 as an entrée • Preparation 20 mins • Cook 2¼ hours • Cooker capacity 1.5 litres

Pinch of saffron
1 tablespoon warm water
2 cups full cream (whole) milk
2 tablespoons cornflour (cornstarch)
1 teaspoon curry powder
1 extra tablespoon cornflour (cornstarch), mixed to a slurry with 1 tablespoon
    water (optional)
16 large raw prawns (shrimp), heads and shells removed, deveined
Steamed rice, to serve

1. Crush the saffron with a wooden spoon and soak it in the warm water for 10 minutes.

2. Whisk the milk, cornflour, curry powder and saffron mixture together in a bowl. Transfer to the slow cooker, cover and cook on low for 2 hours. Whisk the mixture occasionally to remove lumps.

3. Check the consistency of the sauce, and if it's not thick enough, add the cornflour slurry and stir well to combine.

4. Add the prawns and cook for 15 minutes on high or until the prawns have changed colour and are cooked through.

5. Serve with steamed rice.

Asian Inspired Fish Fillets

The first time I cooked this recipe, everyone in my family begged me to make it again the very next night – a double batch! They couldn't get enough of it. I make this using packaged frozen basa fillets from the supermarket. Perfect with a salad or hot chips.

Serves 4 • Preparation 10 mins • Cook 2 hours • Cooker capacity 6 litres

1 kg (2 lb 3 oz) white fish fillets (I use basa)
1 tablespoon soy sauce
1 tablespoon sweet chilli sauce
1 teaspoon sesame oil
1 teaspoon minced ginger
1 teaspoon brown sugar
½ cup sliced spring onions (scallions)

1. Line the slow cooker with baking paper and arrange the fish on the baking paper.

2. Combine all the other ingredients except the spring onions in a jug. Sprinkle the liquid over the fish fillets. Scatter with spring onions.

3. Cook on high for 2 hours (see note), basting the fish occasionally with the cooking liquid.

4. Remove the fish carefully with an egg flip so as not to break the soft fillets.

NOTE: The fish is cooked when you can easily flake pieces off with a fork. The timing depends on the thickness of the fillets.

Crumbed Fish Cakes

When you cook crumbed food in the slow cooker, you don't need to add fat or oil – I love that! Not only is it healthier than deep-frying, but there's no chance of burning anything if you turn your back for a moment. Serve these with vegetables, or in a burger with salad.

Serves 6 • Preparation 20 mins • Cook 3½ hours • Cooker capacity 7 litres

Oil spray, for greasing
425 g (15 oz) can tuna in springwater, drained very well, flaked
260 g (9 oz) mashed potato (see note)
1 egg, beaten
2 tablespoons extra sharp shredded parmesan cheese
2 tablespoons mayonnaise
1 tablespoon minced garlic
1 tablespoon Dijon mustard
1 teaspoon cracked black pepper
½ teaspoon salt
½–1 cup fine dry breadcrumbs, for coating

1. Line the base of the slow cooker with baking paper and spray lightly with oil.

2. Combine all the ingredients except the breadcrumbs and oil spray in a bowl and mix well.

3. Place the breadcrumbs in a separate bowl.

4. Roll the tuna mixture into golf ball–sized balls (about 12) using your hands.

5. Working with one ball at a time, flatten slightly, then press both sides into breadcrumbs to coat. Set aside on a plate and repeat with remaining balls.

6. Arrange the fish cakes on the baking paper in a single layer.

7. Cover, putting a tea towel (dish towel) under the lid, and cook on high for about 3½ hours, turning halfway through the cooking time (see note).

NOTE: When you make mashed potato for this recipe, there's no need to add any butter or milk.

Keep an eye on the fish cakes, and when they are golden on the base, turn them over. Make that the halfway point of your cooking time.

Mediterranean Fish Fillets

As a child, I spent all the holidays and many weekends on Fraser Island. My parents were mad keen on fishing, so I ate a lot of fish. A lot! This meant that as an adult, I went for 20-odd years choosing not to cook it or eat it. That is, until I started slow-cooking it. It's impossible to go wrong with slow-cooked fish, and it opens up a lot more options than the traditional crumbed, battered and grilled fish I grew up with. The rich tomato and basil flavours in this recipe are to die for.

Serves 4 • Preparation 15 mins • Cook 2 hours • Cooker capacity 6 litres

1 kg (2 lb 3 oz) basa fillets
1 large red onion, diced
100 g (3½ oz) tomato pesto
10 grape or cherry tomatoes, halved

1. Line the slow cooker with baking paper. Place the fish on the paper and scatter with onion.
2. Combine the pesto with ¼ cup water and pour the mixture over the fish. Scatter with tomato.
3. Cover, putting a tea towel (dish towel) under the lid, and cook on high for 2 hours or until the fish is cooked through.
4. Transfer carefully to serving plates using an egg flip – the fish will be very fragile.
5. Spoon some of the pesto sauce over the fish and garnish with the tomato.

Creamy Garlic Seafood Medley

I use a seafood marina mix from the seafood counter of the supermarket deli for this recipe; it includes fish, prawns, mussels and calamari. But choose your own fresh seafood assortment if you prefer. Whatever you select, you'll love it cooked in this indulgent creamy garlic sauce.

Serves 2 • Preparation 15 mins • Cook 2 hours • Cooker capacity 1.5 litres

500 g (1 lb 2 oz) seafood marina mix (fish, prawns, mussels, calamari)
300 ml (10 fl oz) cooking cream
1 tablespoon minced garlic
½ teaspoon mustard powder
½ teaspoon white pepper
2 tablespoons cornflour (cornstarch), mixed to a slurry with 2 tablespoons water
Rice or pasta, to serve

1. Combine all the ingredients except the cornflour slurry in the slow cooker and stir well.

2. Cover and cook on high for 1 hour 50 minutes.

3. Stir in the cornflour slurry and cook for another 10 minutes to thicken the sauce.

4. Serve on rice or pasta.

Seafood Marinara Fettuccine

This is a classic mixed seafood selection in a tomato-based sauce. It looks amazing and tastes it too. If you don't have fettuccine on hand, you can use any other pasta.

Serves 2 • Preparation 15 mins • Cook 2 hours • Cooker capacity 1.5 litres

500 g (1 lb 2 oz) seafood marina mix (fish, prawns, mussels, calamari)
400 g (14 oz) can diced Italian tomatoes
1 onion, finely chopped
2 tablespoons fresh parsley, chopped
1 clove garlic, minced
½ teaspoon cracked black pepper
Fettuccine, to serve

1. Combine all the ingredients in the slow cooker.

2. Cover and cook on high for 2 hours.

3. Serve with fettuccine.

Lemon and Garlic Butter Scallops

When I first made these scallops, I almost missed out on tasting them. I'd called my children to come and try some, and then turned my back for a second. When I turned around, there were only three scallops left on the plate – they'd swarmed like seagulls and devoured almost all of them! It's safe to say they LOVED them and have requested them several times since. In future, I'll put mine aside before I call them.

Serves 2 as a generous entrée • Preparation 15 mins • Cook ¾ hour
• Cooker capacity 3.5 litres

300 g (10½ oz) scallops
3 tablespoons butter, melted
1½ tablespoons fresh lemon juice
3 garlic cloves, minced, or ½ tablespoon minced garlic
1 teaspoon dried parsley

1. Place the scallops in the slow cooker.

2. Combine all the other ingredients in a bowl, then pour the mixture over the scallops.

3. Cover, putting a tea towel (dish towel) under the lid, and cook on high for 40–45 minutes or until the scallops are cooked through.

Crustless Crab Quiche

Growing up in Hervey Bay, I was lucky to be raised eating mud crabs that my Dad caught on Fraser Island. These days I'm not so lucky as to enjoy fresh crab very often, so using canned crab meat or seafood extender is a budget-friendly alternative. This quiche looks and sounds fancy, but requires minimal effort. The proof is in the tasting – so good! You could make this mixture into mini quiches in silicone muffin cases, or in one large block to be cut into small squares.

Serves 4 • Preparation 10 mins • Cook 1 hour • Cooker capacity 7 litres

4 eggs
½ cup thickened (whipping) cream
1 cup fresh or canned crab meat (or seafood extender)
⅔ cup grated Swiss cheese
12 chives, chopped
¼ teaspoon garlic powder
Oil spray, for greasing

1. Whisk the eggs and cream together in a mixing bowl. Cut the crab meat or seafood extender into thin ribbons and stir through.

2. Add the cheese, chives and garlic powder. Season with salt and pepper and stir to combine.

3. Spray a silicone flan dish (or whatever you wish to cook your quiche in) well with oil. Pour the mixture into the prepared dish and carefully place it in the slow cooker.

4. Cover, putting a tea towel (dish towel) under the lid, and cook on high for 1 hour or until set.

NOTE: You could also cook this directly in your slow cooker on a lining of baking paper.

PORK

Honey Soy and Garlic Pork Ribs

As someone only recently converted to cooking and eating ribs, I am certainly making up for lost time! How good are ribs? So good! Honey, soy and garlic flavours complement these perfectly – they're finger licking good served with slaw and couscous or sweet potato wedges.

Serves 4–6 • Preparation 15 mins • Cook 6–7 hours • Cooker capacity 6 litres

1.5 kg (3 lb 5 oz) pork ribs
½ cup honey
1½ tablespoons soy sauce
1½ tablespoons lemon juice
1 tablespoon minced garlic

1. Place the ribs in the slow cooker. Combine all the other ingredients in a bowl and pour the mixture over the ribs.
2. Cover and cook on low for 6–7 hours, basting occasionally with the sauce.

Sweet Barbecue-style Pork Fillet

Pork fillets are so easy to prep and serve, and the result here is tasty slices of pork in a sweet barbecue sauce. This is lovely served with fried rice and Asian greens.

Serves 5 • Preparation 15 mins • Cook 4–5 hours • Cooker capacity 5 litres

1.5 kg (3 lb 5 oz) pork fillets
½ cup tomato sauce
⅓ cup honey
1 tablespoon soy sauce
1 teaspoon mustard powder
1 tablespoon malt vinegar
1 tablespoon brown sugar
1 tablespoon cornflour (cornstarch), mixed to a slurry with 1 tablespoon water

1. Place the pork in the slow cooker. Combine all the other ingredients except the cornflour slurry, and pour the mixture over the pork.

2. Cover and cook on low for 3¾–4¾ hours or until the pork is very tender.

3. Stir in the cornflour slurry and cook for 15 minutes or until the sauce has thickened.

Char Siu Style Roast Pork

Roast pork with a difference! The flavours of char sui work beautifully with fried rice and Asian vegetables. You'll need to start this recipe a day ahead to marinate the pork.

Serves 6 • Preparation 15 mins (plus marinating) • Cook 8 hours • Cooker capacity 6 litres

1 large piece pork roast, about 1.5 kg (3 lb 5 oz)
⅓ cup hoisin sauce
⅓ cup honey
⅓ cup salt-reduced soy sauce
2 tablespoons rice wine vinegar
2 tablespoons brown sugar
1 tablespoon minced garlic
1½ teaspoons red food colouring
½ teaspoon Chinese five spice

1. Leave the fat and skin on the pork, but remove any netting. Place the pork in a large ziplock bag or oven bag.

2. Combine all the other ingredients in a bowl and pour the mixture into the bag with the pork. Tie, twist or ziplock the bag to seal it, and place it in a large bowl to catch any leaks. Refrigerate overnight to marinate.

3. The next day, remove the pork from the bag and place it in the slow cooker with the rind or fat facing up. Pour the marinade over the pork.

4. Cover and cook on low for 6 hours.

5. Remove the fat/rind layer from the pork and discard it. Turn the pork over and cook for another 2 hours.

6. Serve the pork in slices with the cooking juices spooned over.

Hawaiian Ham Steaks

Ham steaks topped with pineapple, cheese and barbecue sauce make an easy, budget-friendly, summer-style fun family meal. Serve them with salad or on burgers. Delicious!

Serves 4 • Preparation 15 mins • Cook ¾–1 hour • Cooker capacity 6 litres

8 thick-cut ham steaks
Barbecue sauce, to taste
8 slices canned pineapple
8 slices tasty cheese

1. Line the bottom of the slow cooker with baking paper. I use two large cookers for lots of surface area, but you can scale the recipe down to fit your cooker.

2. Arrange the ham steaks in a single layer on the baking paper and drizzle some barbecue sauce on each one.

3. Top each steak with a slice of pineapple and a slice of cheese.

4. Cover, putting a tea towel (dish towel) under the lid, and cook on high for ¾–1 hour or until the cheese is nicely melted.

Barbecue Plum Pork Ribs

I'd never cooked ribs until recently, and now I can't get enough of them! This recipe combines plum and barbecue sauces, two of my favourite flavours, for tasty ribs that will leave you licking your fingers and wanting more.

Serves 4-6 • Preparation 15 mins • Cook 6-7 hours • Cooker capacity 6 litres

2 racks pork ribs (about 1.5 kg (3 lb 5 oz))
½ cup plum sauce
2 tablespoons barbecue sauce
1 tablespoon soy sauce
1 tablespoon sweet chilli sauce
Salad and sweet potato wedges, to serve

1. Place the ribs in the slow cooker.

2. Combine the remaining ingredients and pour the sauce over the ribs.

3. Cover and cook on low for 6–7 hours or until the ribs are very tender, turning them carefully halfway through the cooking time if you're home.

4. Serve with a fresh salad and sweet potato wedges

NOTE: If you're cooking more ribs, just double the sauce mixture.

Pork Steaks in Pepper Sauce

This recipe uses thin schnitzel-style pork steaks for a fast, filling main meal. The canned green peppercorns aren't overly hot, so the recipe is suitable for small children, but if they really don't like them they can pick them out. Serve this with mashed potato to go with the creamy sauce, and steamed vegetables.

Serves 4 • Preparation 15 mins • Cook 2 hours • Cooker capacity 5 litres

800 g (1 lb 12 oz) thin pork schnitzels (about 12; see note)
1 small onion, finely diced
300 ml (10 fl oz) cooking cream
55 g (2 oz) can green peppercorns, drained
1 tablespoon minced garlic
2 teaspoons beef stock powder
2 tablespoons cornflour (cornstarch), mixed to a slurry with 2 tablespoons water

1. Place the pork in the slow cooker and top with the onion. Combine all the other ingredients except the cornflour slurry and pour the mixture over the steaks. Stir to coat the pork in the sauce.

2. Cover and cook on high for 1¾ hours.

3. Stir in the cornflour slurry and cook for another 15 minutes.

NOTE: Pork schnitzels, or pork minute steaks, are very thin. If you use pork chops or thick steaks, you will need to increase the cooking time to ensure they are thoroughly cooked through. I recommend 5–6 hours on low for those thicker cuts.

Pigs in Blankets

My children can't get enough of these little piggies, and between you and me, neither can I. I could eat just about anything wrapped in bacon with barbecue sauce, and these little pork sausages – oh me oh my! So tasty! A great addition to a party food table or your next barbecue, too.

Makes 12 • Preparation 20 mins • Cook 4–5 hours • Cooker capacity 6 litres

12 pork chipolata sausages (half length sausages)
12 streaky bacon rashers
2 tablespoons tomato sauce (ketchup)
1 tablespoon Dijon mustard
Toothpicks, to secure

1. Line the base of the slow cooker with baking paper.
2. Wrap each sausage in a rasher of bacon and secure with a toothpick. Place the sausages in the slow cooker.
3. Combine the tomato sauce and mustard and brush the mixture over the sausages with a pastry brush.
4. Cover, putting a tea towel (dish towel) under the lid, and cook on low for 4–5 hours.

NOTE: These will have a richer colour underneath than on the top, so turn them over to serve them.

Saucy Pulled Pork

Before I started slow cooking, I'd never heard of the pulled meat craze. Then I made saucy pulled pork and I haven't looked back. This dish is so versatile. You can serve it with mash and veg, on bread rolls with coleslaw, or even on tortillas with salad. If you want to reduce the sodium content, use salt-reduced sauces.

Serves 4 • Preparation 5 mins • Cook 6 hours • Cooker capacity 6 litres

1 kg (2 lb 4 oz) pork shoulder chops (see note)
¼ cup hoisin sauce
¼ cup barbecue sauce
¼ cup soy sauce
¼ cup sweet chilli sauce
¼ cup tomato sauce (ketchup)
¼ cup Worcestershire sauce
4 garlic cloves, minced
Bread rolls and coleslaw or mashed potato and steamed vegetables, to serve

1. Place the pork in the slow cooker. Combine the remaining ingredients in a bowl with ½ cup water and pour the mixture over the pork.

2. Cover and cook on low for 6 hours.

3. Pull the pork into shreds. You can do this in the slow cooker using plastic non-scratch utensils, or on a cutting board. The long, slow cooking means the meat can be pulled apart very easily.

4. Return the meat to the slow cooker and stir to coat it in the sauce.

5. Serve on bread rolls with coleslaw or with mashed potato and steamed vegetables.

NOTE: You can use a large piece of roasting pork if you prefer. Increase the cooking time to 8 hours.

Simple 'n' Saucy Pork Chops

I decided I wanted to expand my pork repertoire, so I came up with this recipe for pork chops that takes only minutes to whip up. I'm a die-hard barbecue sauce fan, as is everyone in my family, so we love this recipe. We serve it with crunchy French fries and a large side salad.

Serves 4 • Preparation 5 mins • Cook 4 hours • Cooker capacity 6 litres

4 pork chops
1 onion, diced
1 cup tomato sauce (ketchup)
½ cup barbecue sauce
½ cup (lightly packed) light brown sugar

1. Place the pork in the slow cooker in a single layer and put the onion on top.
2. Combine the remaining ingredients in a bowl and pour the mixture over the chops.
3. Cover and cook on low for 3 hours.
4. Place a tea towel (dish towel) under the lid and continue cooking for 1 hour.
5. Serve the chops with the sauce spooned over.

NOTE: You can easily increase the number of chops for more serves, as the recipe makes plenty of sauce.

Sweet Chilli Pork Chops

This is one of my favourite pork chop recipes. The sauce is mild enough for the whole family but you could increase the heat factor with a hotter sweet chilli sauce if you prefer. You can increase the number of pork chops to suit your family as the recipe makes plenty of sauce. Use whatever cut of pork chop you prefer, or whatever is on special at your butcher to keep it within your budget. We like this with mashed potato and vegetables, as the sauce is divine spooned over the mash.

Serves 6 • Preparation 10 mins • Cook 6 hours • Cooker capacity 6 litres

6 pork chops
1 large onion, thinly sliced
½ cup mild sweet chilli sauce
¼ cup hoisin sauce
1 tablespoon minced garlic
1 teaspoon sesame oil

1. Place the pork in the slow cooker and scatter the onion on top. Combine the remaining ingredients in a bowl and pour the mixture over the pork.

2. Cover and cook on low for 6 hours.

NOTE: If the sauce is too runny, transfer the pork chops to serving plates and keep warm. Increase the slow cooker to high. Mix 1 tablespoon cornflour (cornstarch) with 1 tablespoon water until smooth. Add to the slow cooker and cook, stirring, for about 5 minutes or until thickened.

Mexican Pulled Pork Sliders

Saucy pulled pork is great for parties and entertaining – your guests can serve themselves. It's also easy to present on sliders with a fresh crunchy slaw, and if your kids are anything like mine they love any dinner on bread rolls! With only three ingredients, this is simple enough for the kids to make under your supervision.

Serves 10–12 • Preparation 10 mins • Cook 9 hours • Cooker capacity 6 litres

1.5 kg (3 lb 5 oz) piece boneless pork
400 g (14 oz) can diced tomatoes
2 x 30 g (1 oz) packets reduced-salt taco seasoning
Bread rolls and crunchy slaw, to serve

1. Leave the fat on the pork. Place the pork in the slow cooker, fat-side down. Pour the tomatoes over and sprinkle with the taco seasoning.

2. Cover and cook on low for 9 hours.

3. Carefully turn the pork over. Remove the fat layer from the pork and discard it.

4. Pull the pork into shreds. You can do this in the slow cooker using plastic non-scratch utensils, or on a cutting board. The long, slow cooking means the meat can be pulled apart very easily.

5. Return the meat to the slow cooker and stir to coat it in the sauce.

6. Serve on bread rolls with crunchy slaw.

Sweet and Sour Pork Rashers

This sweet and sour flavour-packed pork recipe was a huge hit with our kids! I served it with brown rice and steamed broccolini for high fives all round.

Serves 5 • Preparation 20 mins • Cook 5 hours • Cooker capacity 6 litres

1 kg (2 lb 3 oz) pork rashers
1 tablespoon oil
½ red capsicum (pepper), sliced
½ green capsicum (pepper), sliced
¾ cup sugar
½ cup salt-reduced soy sauce
½ cup white vinegar
½ cup canned crushed pineapple
2 tablespoons yellow mustard
1 heaped teaspoon minced garlic
1 heaped teaspoon minced ginger
Brown rice and steamed broccolini, to serve

1. Cut the pork rashers into thirds. Heat the oil in a frying pan over medium-high heat. Cook the pork rashers for about 5 minutes, turning once, until sealed. Transfer to the slow cooker.

2. Add the capsicum. Combine the remaining ingredients and pour into the slow cooker. Season with salt and pepper.

3. Cover and cook on high for 4–5 hours. Put a tea towel (dish towel) under the lid for the last hour of cooking, which will help to thicken the sauce a little by absorbing excess moisture.

4. Served with brown rice and steamed broccolini

NOTE: I drizzle only a little of the sauce over the pork when serving because it's high in sugar, but you could use as much as you like.

Creamy Pepper Pork Chops

The lovely peppery sauce with these pork chops has a bit of bite so you may wish to tone it down by reducing the amount of pepper for the young or faint-hearted.

Serves 4 • Preparation 5 mins • Cook 4–6 hours • Cooker capacity 5 litres

4 pork chops, rind and excess fat trimmed
1 onion, finely diced
2 garlic cloves, minced
1 teaspoon salt-reduced beef stock powder
1 teaspoon freshly ground black pepper, or to taste
420 g (15 oz) can condensed cream of mushroom soup
Baby potatoes or mashed potato, steamed peas and carrots, to serve

1. Place the pork chops in the slow cooker. Scatter the onion, garlic, stock powder and pepper over the chops. Pour over the soup. Cover and cook on low for 4–6 hours.

2. Serve the pork chops with the creamy sauce and baby potatoes or mash with peas and carrots.

Cheese and Salami Sticks

These hot, cheesy, delicious little pastry parcels are great for a party. I use salami made from pork, but you can use any kind you like.

Makes 8 • Preparation 10 mins • Cook 1½ hours • Cooker capacity 6 litres

Oil spray, for greasing
2 sheets puff pastry
8 slices shaved mild salami
8 cheese sticks
1 egg, whisked

1. Spray the slow cooker bowl with oil spray.

2. Cut each sheet of pastry into four squares. Place a salami slice and a cheese stick on each square. Roll up each square into a cylinder to enclose the filling. Pinch the ends closed.

3. Prick the top of each parcel twice with a fork to allow steam to escape during cooking. Brush the parcels with beaten egg and place in the slow cooker.

4. Cover, putting a tea towel (dish towel) under the lid, and cook on high for 1¼ hours.

5. Turn over and cook for another 15 minutes.

6. Serve – be careful, the cheese filling will be hot!

MINCE &
MEATBALLS

Glazed Mini Meatloaves

Bite-sized meatloaves are great for parties, barbecues, kids' lunches and even easy finger food for toddlers. You'll need 18 silicone muffin cases for this recipe or a muffin pan that fits in your slow cooker.

Makes 18 • Preparation 25 mins • Cook 2½ hours • Cooker capacity 7 litres

MEATLOAF
1 kg (2 lb 3 oz) minced (ground) beef
1 cup fine breadcrumbs
1 small egg
1 small onion, grated
¼ cup tomato sauce (ketchup)
2 tablespoons Worcestershire sauce
1 tablespoon minced garlic
2 teaspoons dried Italian herb blend
½ teaspoon salt
½ teaspoon cracked black pepper

GLAZE
¼ cup tomato sauce (ketchup)
1 tablespoon brown sugar
1 tablespoon Dijon mustard

1. For the meatloaf, combine all the ingredients in a large mixing bowl. Mix well using your hands.

2. Form the mixture into 18 balls and place each ball in a muffin or cupcake case.

3. For the glaze, combine all the ingredients. Brush the glaze on the top of each meatloaf with a spoon or pastry brush.

4. Arrange the meatloaves in a single layer in the slow cooker.

5. Cover and cook on high for 2½ hours.

6. Cool slightly, then remove meatloaves from cases to serve.

NOTES: Some excess oil from the beef might accumulate in the cupcake cases during cooking. Tip it out and discard it before serving the meatloaves.

⚓— Creamy Beef and Pasta —⚓

I LOVE one-pot meals – they take the convenience of slow cooking to the next level. Simply serve and dinner is done! The only thing I suggest adding to this meal is a buttered bread roll (you can thank me later). This creamy pasta dish is a huge hit with the little ones in my house, and most of them go back for seconds – it's that popular.

Serves 5 • Preparation 15 mins • Cook 4¾ hours • Cooker capacity 5 litres

1 kg (2 lb 3 oz) minced (ground) beef
700 ml (24 fl oz) bottle tomato passata (puréed tomato)
1 large onion, diced
½ cup water
1 chorizo sausage, chopped
2 teaspoons beef stock powder
2 garlic cloves, minced
1½ cups small pasta shapes (I use dinosaur shapes for the kids)
300 ml (10 fl oz) cooking cream
Buttered crusty bread rolls, to serve

1. Combine all the ingredients except the pasta and cream in the slow cooker. Cover and cook on low for 4 hours.

2. Add the pasta and cream and cook for 45 minutes or until the pasta is cooked through.

3. Serve with buttered crusty bread rolls.

Sweet and Sour Pork Mince

This pork mince recipe is easy on the tastebuds and easy on the wallet. It's delicious with rice and vegetables, or even on burgers.

Serves 4 • Preparation 15 mins • Cook 5 hours • Cooker capacity 5 litres

500 g (1 lb 2 oz) minced (ground) pork
440 g (15½ oz) can pineapple pieces in juice, drained, juice discarded
1 small red chilli, deseeded and finely diced
2 tablespoons minced ginger
1 tablespoon minced garlic
1 red capsicum (pepper), diced
¼ cup brown sugar
¼ cup rice wine vinegar
¼ cup oyster sauce
2 tablespoons soy sauce

1. Combine all the ingredients in the slow cooker.

2. Cover and cook on low for 5 hours.

NOTE: I don't thicken the mince with cornflour, because I serve it with rice to soak up the sauce. If you'd prefer it thicker, stir in 1 tablespoon of cornflour mixed with 1 tablespoon of cornflour 10 minutes before the end of the cooking time.

Mexican Mince and Potato Bake

I live in a household of Mexican-food lovers, and I confess we enjoy a great potato bake too. So one day I decided to combine these two favourites. Serve this with a dollop of sour cream, and guacamole too if you like, for a one-pot cheesy Mex meal the whole family will enjoy.

Serves 4 • Preparation 15 mins • Cook 6 hours • Cooker capacity 5 litres

1 kg (2 lb 3 oz) potatoes, skin on
1 kg (2 lb 3 oz) minced (ground) beef
435 g (15½ oz) can refried beans
40 g (1½ oz) sachet taco seasoning or other Mexican seasoning
2 cups grated tasty cheese
Sour cream, to serve

1. Chop the potatoes into pieces about half the size of a golf ball. Place them in the slow cooker.
2. Combine the mince, beans and seasoning in a large bowl. Spread the mixture over the potatoes and smooth the top.
3. Cover and cook on low for 5¾ hours.
4. Sprinkle the cheese over the top and cook for another 15 minutes.
5. Serve with a dollop of sour cream for a one-pot Mexican meal.

▤— Hamburger Helpers —●

This method not only makes burgers easy to cook, it also stops all the fillings from sliding out of the bun when you start eating. Melted cheese locks in the sauce, mushrooms and onion. Add some lettuce and it's 2,4,6,8, tuck in – don't wait! You can easily wrap them up for lunches, picnics and even sports games.

Serves 6 • Preparation 10 mins • Cook 2 hours 15mins • Cooker capacity 6 litres

6 hamburger patties
6 tablespoons smoky barbecue sauce
½–1 small onion, sliced
3 large mushrooms, sliced
6 cheese slices
Burger rolls and salad leaves, to serve

1. Line the slow cooker with baking paper. Arrange the burger patties in a single layer on the paper.
2. Top each burger with a spoonful of sauce, then add the onion and mushroom slices.
3. Cover, putting a tea towel (dish towel) under the lid, and cook on high for 2 hours or until the meat is cooked through.
4. Top each burger with a slice of cheese and cook for another 15 minutes to melt the cheese.
5. Remove the burgers carefully using an egg flip (everything stays together thanks to the cheese) and place each one on half a bread roll.
6. Top with salad leaves, sandwich with the roll tops, and serve.

NOTE: It's easy to adapt the toppings as you like. We leave the mushrooms out of our kids' burgers and add extra ones to ours.

Beef Nachos

Who doesn't love nachos – na-yum-chos! Spoon the delicious Mexican mince mix over your favourite corn chips, add cheese and sour cream and away you go. The refried beans add the Mexican flavour you're looking for, and as a bonus they make this meal go further for minimal cost.

Serves 6 • Preparation 20 mins • Cook 5 hours • Cooker capacity 3.5 litres

MEXICAN MINCE
500 g (1 lb 2 oz) minced (ground) beef
435g (15½ oz) can refried beans
½ cup canned red kidney beans, rinsed and drained
400g (14 oz) can diced tomatoes
2 tablespoons tomato paste (concentrated purée)
1 teaspoon chilli powder (see note)
1 teaspoon ground cumin
1 teaspoon paprika
½ teaspoon onion powder
½ teaspoon garlic powder
½ teaspoon dried oregano

TO SERVE
Corn chips
Grated cheese
Sour cream
Mashed avocado

1. To make the Mexican mince, combine all the ingredients in the slow cooker. Cover and cook on low for 5 hours.

2. To serve, arrange the corn chips on serving plates. Spoon over some Mexican mince and top with grated cheese (see note). Add a dollop of sour cream and smashed avocado.

NOTES: We like to zap the nachos in the microwave for 30–60 seconds per plate to melt the cheese nicely before adding the rest of the toppings, but this is optional. The cheese will melt a little of its own accord anyway.

You can replace the six spices with a 40 g (1½ oz) packet of taco seasoning if you prefer to make an easier version.

━━ Salisbury Steak ━●

I confess I used to think Salisbury steak was actually a 'steak' recipe, not something involving oversized rissoles (meat patties) in a lush gravy. Once I worked it out, I knew right away my children would love it. Tip: have some bread on hand to wipe up all the sauce, because you won't want to leave any on your plate.

Serves 6 • Preparation 20 mins • Cook 5–6 hours • Cooker capacity 6 litres

GRAVY
½ onion, sliced
500 g (1 lb 2 oz) mushrooms, sliced
2 cups beef stock
30 g (1 oz) sachet traditional style gravy powder
1 tablespoon Worcestershire sauce
1 teaspoon mustard

STEAK
1 kg (2 lb 3 oz) minced (ground) beef
½ onion, grated
1 egg
1 teaspoon beef stock powder or 1 beef stock cube
⅔ cup breadcrumbs
2 tablespoons tomato sauce (ketchup)
1 tablespoon Worcestershire sauce
1 teaspoon mustard

1. Prepare the gravy first. Combine the onion and mushroom in the slow cooker. Combine all the other gravy ingredients in a bowl, whisk well, and add to the slow cooker. Set aside.

2. To make the 'steak', combine all the ingredients in a large mixing bowl. Mix well with your hands. Shape the mixture into 12 large rissoles (meat patties).

3. Place the rissoles carefully on top of the onion and mushroom in the slow cooker, ideally in a single layer.

4. Cover, putting a tea towel (dish towel) under the lid, and cook on low for 5–6 hours or until the meat is cooked through.

5. Transfer the steak to a plate, cover with foil and keep warm.

6. Transfer the gravy to a saucepan and simmer on the stovetop over medium–high heat until slightly reduced and thickened. (If you have a searing insert in your slow cooker, you can use this.)

7. Serve the steak beside mashed potato, with the gravy spooned over.

Mini Muffin Pizza Cups

These are a fun meal for kids or a great party food. Each little muffin cup has the taste of a mini pizza on a chicken mince base. You could vary the toppings to re-create your own favourite pizza flavours. You'll need 12 silicone muffin cases for this recipe, or a muffin tray that fits in your slow cooker.

Makes 12 • Preparation 20 mins • Cook 2 hours • Cooker capacity 6 litres

500 g (1 lb 2 oz) minced (ground) chicken
Salt and pepper, to taste
½–¾ cup pizza sauce (tomato or barbecue style)
½ cup diced green capsicum (pepper)
½ cup diced red onion
2 cups pizza-style grated cheese blend (mozzarella, cheddar and parmesan)

1. Divide the chicken mince between the muffin cases and press to form pizza bases. Season to taste with salt and pepper.

2. Spread each base with 1–2 teaspoons pizza sauce. Top with capsicum and onion.

3. Arrange the muffin cases in the slow cooker in a single layer. Cover, putting a tea towel (dish towel) under the lid, and cook on high for 1½ hours.

4. Divide the cheese between the muffin cases. Cook for another 30 minutes or until the cheese is melted and the chicken is cooked through.

5. Serve hot.

Mexican Potato Gem Casserole

Serve this casserole with a dollop of sour cream and some mashed avocado for a Mexican taste sensation. There's no need to pre-brown the minced meat, but if you do, reduce the initial cooking time to 1 hour.

Serves 4 • Preparation 10 mins • Cook 6 hours • Cooker capacity 6 litres

1 kg (2 lb 3 oz) lean minced (ground) beef
420 g (15 oz) can diced tomatoes
2 tomatoes, diced
1 red onion, diced
1 green capsicum (pepper), diced
1–2 x 40 g (1½ oz) sachets taco seasoning
1 kg (2 lb) packet frozen potato gems (tater tots)
¾ cup grated cheese (I use low-fat)
Sour cream and mashed avocado, to serve

1. Put the mince in the slow cooker. Add the canned and fresh tomato, onion, capsicum and taco seasoning and stir to combine. Cook on low for 4 hours.

2. Add the potato gems on top of the mince. Cover and cook on low for 1½ hours.

3. Scatter the grated cheese over the mince and potato gems and cook for 30 minutes.

4. Serve with a dollop of sour cream and a spoonful of mashed avocado.

Savoury Mince

This is the epitome of the throw-in-what-you-have style of slow cooking. Start with the mince and add whatever vegetables you have on hand – frozen or finely diced fresh. No two batches of my savoury mince are ever the same. This recipe can easily be doubled without needing extra cooking time.

Serves 4 • Preparation 10 mins • Cook 6 hours • Cooker capacity 5 litres

500 g (1 lb 2 oz) lean minced (ground) beef
½ tin 450 g (15 oz) can condensed tomato soup
1–2 cups diced mixed vegies (fresh or frozen)
1 onion, diced
2 tablespoons Worcestershire sauce
2 tablespoons barbecue sauce
2 tablespoons tomato sauce (ketchup)
1 tablespoon instant gravy mix (roast meat or brown onion flavour)
2 garlic cloves, minced
1 beef stock cube
Mashed potato and corn on the cob, to serve

1. Combine all the ingredients in the slow cooker with ½ cup water and stir well. Season with salt and freshly ground black pepper. Cover and cook on low for 6 hours.

2. Serve with mashed potato and corn on the cob.

Shepherd's Pie or Cottage Pie

Traditionally, shepherd's pie is cooked with lamb mince and cottage pie is cooked with beef. This recipe can be made with either for whichever pie you want. You could create a dairy-free version by leaving out the cheese, milk and butter. Serve this with steamed broccoli or broccolini.

Serves 6+ • Preparation 15 mins • Cook 4 hours • Cooker capacity 5 litres

Oil spray, for frying
700 g (1 lb 9 oz) lean minced
    (ground) beef or lamb
1 onion, diced
420 g (15 oz) can diced tomatoes
2 large carrots, grated
2 celery stalks, sliced
½ cup dried green peas
½ cup beef stock
1 tablespoon Worcestershire
    sauce

1 heaped tablespoon tomato
    paste (concentrated purée)
2 garlic cloves, minced
1 teaspoon dried thyme
6 large potatoes (I like golden
    delight potatoes for
    mashing), peeled and cut
    into large pieces
60 ml (¼ cup) milk
1 tablespoon butter
150 g (5½ oz) grated tasty cheese
Paprika, to garnish

1. Spray a large frying pan with oil and heat over medium–high heat. Add the mince and onion in batches, breaking up the mince with a wooden spoon, and cook until the mince is browned. Transfer to the slow cooker.

2. Add the tomato, carrot, celery, peas, stock, Worcestershire sauce, tomato paste, garlic and thyme and stir to combine.

3. Cover and cook on high for 1 hour.

4. Meanwhile, cook the potato in a large saucepan of boiling salted water until tender. Drain. Add the milk and butter and mash until smooth.

5. Smooth the top of the meat mixture in the slow cooker. Spoon the mashed potato over the top and spread it out to cover the meat.

6. Cover and cook on low for 3½ hours.

7. Sprinkle the grated cheese over the top and garnish with paprika (it will give the pie a nice brown finish). Cover, putting a tea towel (dish towel) under the lid, and continue cooking for 30 minutes.

Porcupines in Barbecue Sauce

Porcupines were my first-ever slow-cooker fail, back in the day. But I'm nothing if not determined! I'm a barbecue sauce girl through and through, so I knew I had to make a barbecue version if I was going to love them. These turned out even better than I'd hoped, and the whole family enjoyed them. Serve the meatballs over pasta or on their own, with seasonal vegetables.

Makes 24 large meatballs • Preparation 15 mins • Cook 6 hours • Cooker capacity 5 litres

500 g (1 lb 2 oz) lean minced (ground) beef
½ cup long grain white rice (uncooked)
1 large onion, grated
1–2 garlic cloves, minced
Plain (all-purpose) flour, for dusting
420 g (15 oz) can cream of tomato condensed soup
400 g (14 oz) can diced tomatoes
½ cup barbecue sauce
1 tablespoon (firmly packed) light brown sugar

1. Combine the mince, rice, onion and garlic in a large bowl. Season with salt and pepper. Form the mixture into golf ball–sized balls using your hands. Roll each ball lightly in flour to coat. Arrange the balls in the slow cooker in a single layer.

2. Combine the soup, tomatoes, barbecue sauce and sugar in a bowl and mix well. Pour gently over the meatballs.

3. Cover and cook on low for 6 hours. If you need to stir, wait until the meatballs are cooked through and firm, so they don't break up.

Classic Curried Mince

This classic curried mince is very versatile. Serve it with creamy mash, cracked black pepper and a scattering of fresh chives, or use it as a filling for pies, pasties or toasted sandwiches. To make a curried cottage pie, top it with mashed potato or sweet potato and cheese. Alternatively, serve it with seasonal vegetables and crusty bread rolls. So many options with this budget mince base.

Serves 6 • Preparation 10 mins • Cook 4–5 hours • Cooker capacity 5 litres

1 kg (2 lb 3 oz) lean minced (ground) beef
1½ cups beef stock
1 large onion, diced
1 large carrot, finely diced
½ cup tomato sauce (ketchup)
2 tablespoons curry powder
1 tablespoon Worcestershire sauce
1 heaped teaspoon minced garlic
Cracked black pepper, to taste

1. Combine all the ingredients in the slow cooker.
2. Cover and cook on low for 4–5 hours.

NOTE: If you'd like a thicker curried mince, combine 1 tablespoon cornflour with 1 tablespoon water and stir it in 15 minutes before the end of the cooking time.

Italian Meatball Subs

We created this recipe during sports season when our children were playing night games at dinner time. It's so much more affordable than buying food for a large family at the fields, and more nutritious too. It's also great for parties: you can serve the meatballs right from the slow cooker, and guests can assemble their own subs.

Makes 28 meatballs • Preparation 15 mins • Cook 4–5 hours • Cooker capacity 6 litres

MEATBALLS
600 g (1 lb 5 oz) minced (ground) pork and veal (70% pork, 30% veal)
1 egg
1 tablespoon chopped fresh parsley
½ teaspoon salt
1 teaspoon minced garlic
1½ tablespoons finely grated parmesan cheese
⅓ cup panko breadcrumbs

SAUCE
400 g (14 oz) can diced tomatoes with herbs and tomato paste (see note)
1 onion, finely diced
1 tablespoon minced garlic
1 tablespoon chopped fresh basil
1 tablespoon chopped fresh oregano
1 tablespoon chopped fresh parsley
Split hot dog rolls and parmesan cheese, to serve

1. To make the meatballs, combine all the ingredients in a mixing bowl. Roll the mixture into balls using your hands. They should be slightly smaller than a golf ball. Set aside.

2. To make the sauce, combine all the ingredients in the slow cooker.

3. Place the meatballs gently on top of the sauce, but do not stir.

4. Cover and cook on low for 4–5 hours.

5. Serve in hot dog rolls, sprinkled with parmesan.

NOTES: If you can't purchase tomatoes combined with herbs and tomato paste, use a can of diced tomatoes and add 1 teaspoon dried mixed herbs and 1 tablespoon tomato paste (concentrated puree).

Resist the urge to stir the meatballs at all until they've cooked for at least 3 hours, so they remain firmly intact. I flip them over gently in the last hour then leave them again.

Turkey Meatballs

I originally created this recipe for people following a low-carb way of eating. However, my family decided they loved it too, so now we make it for everyone. Serve these meatballs with salad, seasonal veggies or pasta, or even on subs.

Serves 4 • Preparation 20 mins • Cook 1¾ hours • Cooker capacity 6 litres

500 g (1 lb 2 oz) minced (ground) turkey
70 g (2⅓ oz) flax almond baking meal (see note)
1 egg
½–1 teaspoon cracked black pepper
½–1 teaspoon all-purpose seasoning
2 teaspoons butter
300 ml (10 fl oz) cooking cream (see note)
1 tablespoon minced garlic

1. Combine the turkey mince, baking meal, egg and seasonings in a large mixing bowl. Mix well with your hands, then roll into 25 balls about the size of a golf ball.

2. Melt the butter in a searing slow cooker or frying pan. Gently add the meatballs and cook for 10 minutes, carefully turning once during cooking. Don't worry if they aren't evenly browned all over. Transfer the meatballs (or the searing insert) to the slow cooker.

3. Combine the cream and garlic and pour over the meatballs.

4. Cover, putting a tea towel (dish towel) under the lid, and cook on low for 1½ hours.

NOTES: Flax almond baking meal, a blend of ground flaxseed (linseed) and ground almonds, is available from health food shops and some supermarkets. The flaxseed helps to bind the meat mixture. You could substitute almond meal or packaged fine breadcrumbs.

The cooking cream is important because it resists splitting like normal cream.

Rich Gravy Mince

Our kids LOVE this budget-friendly flavoured mince meat, and it's so versatile: you can serve it on bread rolls as sliders, with vegetables, in pies or on toasted sandwiches. Simple ingredients, simple to cook, and tastes like old-school meat pie filling!

Serves 6 • Preparation 10 mins • Cook 4 hours • Cooker capacity 6 litres

1 kg (2 lb 3 oz) minced (ground) beef
2 onions, finely diced
½ cup your favourite gravy powder
2 beef stock cubes, crushed

1. Combine all the ingredients with 1 cup water in the slow cooker.

2. Cover and cook on low for 4 hours, stirring occasionally to separate the mince.

Chicken Potato Pie

I love chicken, EVERYTHING chicken, and our children do too. I wanted to make a chicken version of cottage pie or shepherd's pie, and so this recipe was born. Serve it with steamed greens if you like.

Serves 5 • Preparation 20 mins • Cook 5 hours • Cooker capacity 6 litres

FILLING
700 g (1 lb 9 oz) chicken thigh fillets
500 g (1 lb 2 oz) mixed diced frozen vegetables (or fresh if you prefer)
1 onion, diced
1 heaped tablespoon chicken stock powder
1 tablespoon fresh thyme leaves
1 tablespoon fresh rosemary, chopped
1 tablespoon minced garlic
1 tablespoon mustard
1 teaspoon cracked black pepper
½ teaspoon salt
150 ml (5 fl oz) cooking cream

TOPPING
5 large potatoes, chopped
2 tablespoons butter
Milk, to mash
⅔ cup grated tasty cheese

1. For the filling, place all the ingredients except the cream in the slow cooker. Cover and cook on low for 4 hours. Remove the chicken, shred, then return to the cooker. Stir in the cream and continue cooking on low while you prepare the potato topping.

2. For the topping, cook the potatoes in a saucepan of boiling water until tender. Drain well, then mash with butter and milk to a smooth consistency.

3. Spread the topping over the meat mixture in the slow cooker and smooth the surface. Scatter with grated cheese and cook for 30 minutes on high to melt the cheese.

NOTES: No water is added to the filling, as it makes its own liquid. The cooking cream is important because it resists splitting like normal cream.

Easy Meatballs and Gravy

This meatball recipe is fast and easy, and kids love getting their hands in and rolling the balls. I've used a mixture of pork and veal mince here, but you could use chicken mince and chicken gravy, or pork mince and roast pork gravy – whatever your family likes!

Makes 30 meatballs • **Preparation** 20 mins • **Cook** 4 hours • **Cooker capacity** 6 litres

600 g (1 lb 5 oz) minced (ground) pork and veal (70% pork, 30% veal)
½ cup packaged breadcrumbs
1 egg
Oil spray, for greasing
2 cups gravy (made with instant gravy powder and cold water)

1. Combine the mince, breadcrumbs and egg in a mixing bowl. Mix well with your hands, then roll into balls slightly smaller than a golf ball.

2. Spray the slow cooker bowl with oil and add the meatballs. Pour the gravy over.

3. Cover and cook on low for 4 hours.

Barbecue Bacon Burgers

Bacon and barbecue flavours make a tasty filling for burgers or sliders. This is so easy to make, and inexpensive too. It's a great self-serve option for your next party. If your child is like mine and loves baked beans, they'll LOVE this recipe!

Serves 8–10 • Preparation 15 mins • Cook 5 hours • Cooker capacity 6 litres

1 kg (2 lb 3 oz) minced (ground) beef
440 g (15½ oz) can baked beans in barbecue sauce
250 g (9 oz) diced bacon
1 cup barbecue sauce (I use sugar-free)
1 large onion, diced
1 tablespoon minced garlic
Bread rolls, grated cheese and salad (optional), to serve

1. Combine all the ingredients in the slow cooker and stir well.
2. Cover and cook on low for 5 hours.
3. Serve on bread rolls with grated cheese, and salad if you like.

NOTE: Use any leftovers to create a second meal – very versatile!

Carbonara Chicken Meatballs

Easy creamy chicken carbonara meatballs are perfect to serve on subs, or just with the vegetables of your choice. Kids can even help you make them!

Makes 20 • Preparation 15 mins • Cook 3 hours • Cooker capacity 6 litres

500 g (1 lb 2 oz) minced (ground) chicken
½ cup panko breadcrumbs
2 teaspoons minced garlic
1 teaspoon dried rosemary
1 teaspoon dried thyme
½ teaspoon cracked black pepper
½ teaspoon salt
500 g (1 lb 2 oz) jar of your favourite carbonara sauce

1. Combine all the ingredients except the carbonara sauce in a large mixing bowl. Mix well with your hands, then roll into 20 balls about the size of a golf ball.

2. Pour the carbonara sauce into the slow cooker. Gently place the meatballs in the sauce.

3. Cover, putting a tea towel (dish towel) under the lid, and cook on low for 3 hours. Do not stir the meatballs until the last hour of cooking. Moving them before they are cooked will break them.

EGGS AND OTHER BREAKFAST DISHES

Beans & Bacon Breakfast Mugs with Eggs

When I was growing up, my family called me a 'baked bean kid'. I confess – I'm a lifelong lover of those tasty little beans. So, bacon and eggs with a side of baked beans for breakfast, all from a cup? That's my idea of a dream breakfast!

Serves 3 • Preparation 15 mins • Cook 1¼ hours • Cooker capacity 6 litres

555 g (1 lb 3 oz) can baked beans (use your favourite kind; I like Heinz BBQ)
100 g (3½ oz) diced bacon (see note)
Cracked black pepper, to taste
Garlic powder, to taste
¾ cup grated tasty cheese
3 eggs
3 teaspoons finely chopped chives
Toast soldiers, to serve

1. Line the base of the slow cooker with baking paper or paper towel to protect the surface from being scratched by the mugs.

2. Divide the baked beans between 3 mugs, then add a third of the bacon to each mug. Season to taste with pepper and garlic powder and stir to combine.

3. Place the mugs in the slow cooker. Pour two cups of warm water into the slow cooker around the mugs (it doesn't need to reach any particular height on the mugs).

4. Cover, putting a tea towel (dish towel) under the lid, and cook on high for 45 minutes.

5. Check that the beans and bacon are heated through. Add ¼ cup grated cheese to each mug, crack an egg over the cheese, and sprinkle with chives.

6. Cover, putting the tea towel under the lid, and cook on high for another 30 minutes or until the eggs are cooked to your liking.

7. Enjoy breakfast straight from the mug, with toast soldiers on the side.

NOTES: I use the bacon raw, but you can brown it in a frying pan before adding it to the baked beans if you prefer.
It's easy to alter the quantities to serve more people.

No Fail Filled Omelette

If you're anything like me, you're terrible at making omelettes in a pan. Mine always turn out more like scrambled eggs. So I wanted a foolproof way to make omelettes that I could eat plain or fill with whatever I wanted. This is it! I use a ceramic 6 litre slow cooker, although you can use any size. Just keep in mind that the smaller the surface area, the thicker the omelette, so the longer it will take to cook. If you use a searing slow cooker, it may cook faster. Keep an eye on the omelette the first time you make it, and you'll know how long to allow next time. Then you can put it on to cook, go about your business, and return to a perfect omelette.

Serves 2 • Preparation 10 mins • Cook 1 hour • Cooker capacity 6 litres

Oil spray, for greasing
5 large eggs
½ teaspoon dried mixed herbs
Fillings (optional; see notes)

1. Line the slow cooker with baking paper and spray it with oil spray.
2. Whisk the egg and herbs in a bowl and season with salt and pepper. Pour the mixture into the slow cooker. Add fillings (see notes).
3. Cover, putting a tea towel (dish towel) under the lid, and cook on high for 1 hour.
4. Remove the omelette by using the paper to lift it out of the slow cooker.
5. Add any further fillings you like, fold the omelette in half, and serve.

NOTES: You can add your fillings before you cook the omelette, or after it's cooked (or both). The options are limited only by your imagination. You might like to try:
- sliced mushrooms, garlic and cheese
- tomato and chives
- shredded cooked chicken, sliced shallots, semidried tomato and kecap manis (sweet soy sauce)
- thinly sliced salami or chorizo
- cooked bacon
- basil and diced tomato
- avocado
- tomato relish

If you use meat or seafood, be sure to precook them, because they won't cook through in the time it takes to cook the eggs.

Fast and Warming Porridge

I've never been a porridge fan – until now! Making it in the slow cooker means I can put it on to cook then go about my morning chores, and come back to breakfast made. Now the kids request this for a belly-warming, belly-filling start to the day. Serve it topped with honey, fruit (berries and bananas are especially good), nuts or yoghurt.

Makes 2 large serves or 4 small • Preparation 15 mins • Cook 1 hour 10 minutes • Cooker capacity 1.5 litres

> 2 cups milk (see note)
> 1 cup hot water
> 1 cup quick-cook oats
> 3–4 large fresh medjool dates, pitted and diced
> ½ teaspoon ground cinnamon
> Pinch salt
> Honey, fruit, nuts or yoghurt, to serve (optional)

1. Combine all the ingredients except the toppings in the slow cooker.

2. Cover and cook on high for 1 hour 10 minutes (see note).

3. Serve with your choice of toppings.

NOTE: Use whatever milk you prefer – dairy, soy or almond milk, for example.

Keep any eye on the porridge to make sure there's enough liquid, and add a little extra milk or water if you need to. If you use a larger cooker, the porridge will cook more quickly.

Chicken and Corn Mini Quiches

Many people think of quiche as a lunch or dinner dish, but we love mini quiches for a grab-and-go breakfast option too. The classic pairing of chicken and corn makes these really tasty, and they're a great way to use up leftover cooked chicken. They also work well in the kids' lunchboxes. You'll need 16 silicone muffin cases for this recipe.

Makes 16 • Preparation 15 mins • Cook 1¼ hours • Cooker capacity 7 litres

8 eggs
300 g (10½ oz) can creamed corn
1 cup chopped cooked chicken
125 g (4½ oz) can corn kernels, drained
1 tablespoon chopped fresh chives

1. Whisk the eggs in a mixing bowl. Add the remaining ingredients and stir to combine.

2. Divide the mixture between 16 silicone muffin cases.

3. Cover, putting a tea towel (dish towel) under the lid, and cook on high for 1¼ hours.

NOTES: I use a searing slow cooker. If your slow cooker bowl is ceramic, you might choose to sit the muffin cases in 1cm of water to avoid dry cooking.

If your cooker is small, you might need to cook the quiches in two batches.

You could also cook the mixture as a single large quiche in a silicone flan case, or directly on baking paper in the slow cooker. A single quiche will need a longer cooking time – cook it until the egg is just set.

Quick & Easy Quiche Squares

These quiches make a great healthy addition to school lunches, and they're handy to have on hand as a snack. I've used bacon, capsicum, mushrooms and corn here, but you can use whatever ingredients you like. You can also increase the quantities to make bigger squares. I rarely make two quiches exactly the same.

Makes 24 squares • Preparation 10 mins • Cook 1 hour • Cooker capacity 6 litres

8 eggs
⅓ cup low-fat milk
200 g (7 oz) lean bacon (or ham or cooked chicken), diced
½ red capsicum (pepper), finely diced
⅓ cup corn kernels
4 small mushrooms, finely diced
⅛ red onion, finely diced
2 spring onions (scallions), thinly sliced

1. Whisk the eggs and milk together in a large bowl. Add the remaining ingredients, season with salt and freshly ground black pepper, and stir to combine.
2. Line the slow cooker with baking paper and pour in the egg mixture.
3. Cover, putting a tea towel (dish towel) under the lid, and cook on high for 1 hour, or until the quiche is set.
4. Remove the quiche by using the paper to lift it out of the slow cooker.
5. Serve sliced into small squares.

Morning Mushrooms

Imagine a big, tasty mushroom filled with garlic butter, bacon, tomato and spinach, and topped with melted tasty cheese! You can vary the fillings to fit your taste.

Makes 2 • Preparation 10 mins • Cook ¾–1 hour • Cooker capacity 6 litres

- 2 large flat mushrooms
- 2 teaspoons garlic butter (see note)
- 4 cherry tomatoes, halved
- 6 baby spinach leaves, thinly sliced
- 50 g diced bacon
- ½ cup grated tasty cheese

1. Line the slow cooker with baking paper. Remove the stalk from the mushrooms.

2. Top the mushrooms with garlic butter, tomato, spinach and bacon. Carefully place them in the slow cooker and sprinkle with cheese.

3. Cover, putting a tea towel (dish towel) under the lid, and cook on high for ¾–1 hour, until the mushroom is cooked and the cheese has melted.

NOTE: You can use store-bought garlic butter, or make your own: stir together softened butter and minced garlic to taste.

DESSERTS, CAKES AND SWEETS

Cinnamon Cake with Cinnamon Butter Glaze

This has to be one of the most popular cakes I've ever created in my kitchen. The cake itself is delicious, and the glaze is a mix of buttery flavours and crispy doughnut heaven. This is now on repeat in our house – it's that good!

Serves 16 • Preparation 20 mins • Cook 3 hours • Cooker capacity 5.5 litres

Oil spray, for greasing

CINNAMON CAKE
2 cups self-raising flour
1⅓ cups caster (superfine) sugar
160 g (5½ oz) softened butter
3 eggs, lightly beaten
⅔ cup milk
2 teaspoons vanilla essence
1 teaspoon ground cinnamon
½ teaspoon salt

CINNAMON BUTTER GLAZE
2 tablespoons butter, melted
2 tablespoons caster (superfine) sugar
2 teaspoons ground cinnamon

1. Line the slow cooker with baking paper and spray the sides of the bowl with oil spray (in case the cake rises above the paper).

2. For the cinnamon cake, sift the flour into a large mixing bowl. Add the remaining ingredients and mix well with a wooden spoon for 2 minutes or until well combined. Pour the mixture into the slow cooker and smooth the top.

3. Cover, putting a tea towel (dish towel) under the lid, and cook on high for 3 hours or until a skewer inserted into the cake comes out clean.

4. Remove the cake by using the paper to lift it carefully out of the slow cooker. Set aside on a cooling rack.

5. For the cinnamon butter glaze, combine all the ingredients in a bowl. Brush the glaze over the warm cake.

6. Cool, then slice to serve.

Carrot Cake

A slow-cooked version of a classic cake. Top it with your favourite vanilla cream cheese frosting or enjoy as is.

Serves 10 • Preparation 20 mins • Cook 2¾ hours • Cooker capacity 7 litres

2 cups grated carrot
2 cups self-raising flour
1 cup (firmly packed) brown sugar
¾ cup oil
3 eggs, lightly beaten
⅓ cup coarsely chopped almonds or pecans
1 teaspoon vanilla
1 teaspoon salt
1 teaspoon ground cinnamon
½ teaspoon ground nutmeg
Vanilla cream cheese frosting (optional)

1. Spray a silicone loaf pan with oil spray, or line a metal loaf pan with baking paper.
2. Combine all the ingredients in a large mixing bowl and mix well. Pour the mixture into the prepared pan.
3. Place the cake in the slow cooker. If the bowl of your slow cooker is ceramic, pour water around the cake to a depth of about 1 cm (½ inch) to protect the bowl from cracking.
4. Cover, putting a tea towel (dish towel) under the lid, and cook on high for 2¾ hours or until a skewer inserted into the cake comes out clean.
5. Remove the cake and set aside on a cooling rack to cool completely.
6. Top with your favourite vanilla cream cheese frosting if you like.

Apple Crumble

The classic taste of sweet cooked apples with a simple oat-based crumble on top. Serve with a dollop of ice cream for a tasty family desert.

Serves 6 • Preparation 20 mins • Cook 2 hours • Cooker capacity 5 litres

Oil spray, for greasing
Vanilla ice cream or custard, to serve

APPLE MIX
8 Granny Smith apples, peeled, cored, and diced into 1 cm (½ inch) pieces
½ cup (firmly packed) brown sugar
1½ teaspoons ground cinnamon

CRUMBLE
1½ cups rolled oats
½ cup (firmly packed) brown sugar
½ cup plain (all-purpose) flour
1 teaspoon ground cinnamon
100 g butter, diced into 1 cm (½ inch) pieces

1. Spray the slow cooker bowl with oil spray.

2. For the apple mix, combine all the ingredients in a mixing bowl, then place in the slow cooker.

3. For the crumble, combine all the dry ingredients in a mixing bowl. Rub in the butter with your fingertips until crumbly. Spread the mixture evenly over the apples.

4. Cover, putting a tea towel (dish towel) under the lid, and cook on high for 2 hours or until the apple is tender.

5. Serve with vanilla ice cream or custard.

Raisin Bread and Butter Pudding

Take a traditional bread and butter pudding but add cinnamon and sultanas, and you'll have this delicious dessert that tastes like a pudding version of raisin bread! Beautiful served with vanilla custard or ice cream.

Serves 4 • Preparation 20 mins • Cook 1½ hours • Cooker capacity 5 litres

12 slices brioche
40 g (1½ oz) packet sultanas
395 g (14 oz) can sweetened condensed milk
4 eggs
1 teaspoon cinnamon
1 teaspoon vanilla essence
Vanilla custard or ice cream, to serve

1. Cut each slice of brioche into 9 cubes and place in the slow cooker. Scatter with the sultanas.

2. Whisk all the other ingredients together with ½ cup water in a bowl and pour the mixture over the brioche. Stir gently to coat the bread.

3. Cover, putting a tea towel (dish towel) under the lid, and cook on low for 1½ hours or until the egg mixture is set.

4. Serve with custard or ice cream.

Pear and Banana Muffins

These are so more-ish that you'll finish one and want another. Easy to make, they're a tasty treat for kids' lunchboxes or morning tea.

Makes 22 • Preparation 20 mins • Cook 2 hours 50 mins • Cooker capacity 6 litres

4 cups self-raising flour
1 cup (firmly packed) brown sugar
2 eggs, lightly beaten
1 teaspoon ground cinnamon
1 teaspoon vanilla essence
150 ml (5 fl oz) vanilla yoghurt
½ cup milk
½ cup orange juice
1 large banana, diced into small pieces
1 large ripe pear (or 1 cup canned pear slices), diced into small pieces

1. Combine all the ingredients in a large mixing bowl and mix well.

2. Divide the mixture between 22 silicone muffin cases.

3. Cook the muffins in 2 batches. Place half of them in the slow cooker. If the bowl of your slow cooker is ceramic, pour water around the muffin cases to a depth of about 1 cm (½ inch) to protect the bowl from cracking.

4. Cover, putting a tea towel (dish towel) under the lid, and cook on high for 1 hour 25 minutes or until the muffins spring back when lightly pressed.

5. Repeat with the remaining muffins. The second batch will probably cook more quickly because the cooker is already preheated from the first batch.

Hummingbird Cake with Cream Cheese Frosting

Hummingbird cake was originally created in Jamaica in the 1970s and typically incudes nuts, fruit and frosting. This slow-cooker version is a lovely dense cake and keeps well for lunchboxes. It's especially nice topped with the traditional cream cheese frosting.

Serves 10 • Preparation 20 mins • Cook 2–2½ hours • Cooker capacity 6 litres

200 g (7 oz) drained canned crushed pineapple in juice (weigh after draining)
150 g (5½ oz) butter, softened
⅔ cup self-raising flour
⅔ cup plain (all-purpose) flour
⅔ cup (firmly packed) brown sugar
1 small ripe banana, mashed
2 eggs, lightly beaten
70 g (2½ oz) coarsely chopped walnuts or pecans
1 teaspoon vanilla essence

CREAM CHEESE FROSTING
1⅓ cups icing (confectioner's) sugar
125 g (4½ oz) spreadable cream cheese
30 g (1 oz) butter, softened
1 teaspoon vanilla essence

1. Spray a silicone loaf pan with oil spray, or line a metal loaf pan with baking paper.

2. Combine all the ingredients in a mixing bowl and mix well. Pour the mixture into the prepared pan.

3. Place the cake in the slow cooker. If the bowl of your slow cooker is ceramic, pour water around the cake to a depth of about 1 cm (½ inch) to protect the bowl from cracking.

4. Cover, putting a tea towel (dish towel) under the lid, and cook on high for 2–2½ hours or until a skewer inserted into the cake comes out clean. (Test the cake after 1½ hours and again after 2 hours.)

5. Meanwhile, make the cream cheese frosting. Combine all the ingredients in a mixing bowl and beat until smooth and creamy. Set aside in the refrigerator.

6. Remove the cake from the slow cooker and set aside on a rack to cool completely.

7. Spread the frosting over the cooled cake.

Double Choc Fudge Brownies

Just let those words sink in: Double. Choc. Fudge. Brownie. Says it all, really, don't you think? #YUM.

Serves 16 • Preparation 15 mins • Cook 1½–2 hours • Cooker capacity 7 litres

Oil spray, for greasing
2 cups plain (all-purpose) flour
1½ cups caster (superfine) sugar
125 g (4½ oz) butter, melted
½ cup cocoa powder
½ cup white chocolate melts or buttons
3 eggs, lightly beaten
1 teaspoon vanilla essence

1. Line the slow cooker with baking paper and give it a light spray with oil.

2. Combine all the ingredients in a large bowl and mix well. Pour the mixture into the slow cooker.

3. Cover, putting a tea towel (dish towel) under the lid, and cook on high for 1½ -2 hours.

4. Set aside to firm and cool slightly before cutting (if you can resist that long, ha ha).

Blueberry Pancake Slab

This slab-type cake, based on a pancake recipe, is great in lunchboxes, for snacks, or with ice cream for dessert.

Serves 16 • Preparation 20 mins • Cook 1¼–1½ hours • Cooker capacity 7 litres

2 cups self-raising flour
1 cup milk
½ cup caster (superfine) sugar
1 egg, lightly beaten
1 tablespoon butter, melted
1 teaspoon vanilla essence
½ teaspoon bicarbonate of soda
125 g (4½ oz) punnet blueberries

1. Line the slow cooker with baking paper.

2. Combine all the ingredients except the blueberries in a large mixing bowl and stir until smooth. Gently stir in the blueberries. Pour the mixture into the slow cooker.

3. Cover, putting a tea towel (dish towel) under the lid, and cook on high for 1¼–1½ hours or until a skewer inserted into the cake comes out clean.

4. Remove the cake by using the paper to lift it carefully out of the slow cooker. Set aside on a cooling rack.

5. Slice into large squares to serve.

Sweet Strawberry & Sultana Scrolls

I wanted something a little different from the usual scroll fillings, so I combined two tastes my kids love: strawberries and sultanas. These are ahhhmazing! Great for lunchboxes and after-school treats.

Serves 8-10 • Preparation 25 mins • Cook 1¾–2¼ hours • Cooker capacity 6 litres

2 cups self-raising flour
¾ cup milk
75 g (2½ oz) butter, melted
Pinch of salt
300 g (10½ oz) strawberry jam (jelly)
40 g (1½ oz) box sultanas
1–2 teaspoons ground cinnamon, to taste

1. Line the slow cooker with baking paper.

2. Combine the flour, milk, butter and salt in a mixing bowl and stir until the dough just comes together. If it's too dry and crumbly, add an extra ¼ cup milk.

3. Turn the dough out onto a lightly floured bench and knead until smooth.

4. Roll out the dough into a 20 x 30 cm (8 x 11 inch) rectangle using a rolling pin.

5. Spread the jam over the dough, then scatter with sultanas and sprinkle with cinnamon.

6. Roll up the dough into a long cylinder.

7. Cut the roll into 8–10 slices with a sharp knife (they will look like little snails when cut). If cutting flattens the scrolls or makes the jam ooze out, reshape them after cutting so they resemble snails.

8. Arrange the scrolls flat in a single layer, close together, in the slow cooker.

9. Cover, putting a tea towel (dish towel) under the lid, and cook on high for 1¾ hours or until the scrolls are cooked through. Some slow cookers will need an extra 15–30 minutes.

10. Serve hot and fresh, or store in the fridge and pack for lunchbox treats.

← Strawberries and Cream Cookies →

Nothing complements strawberries like cream, and these cookies are a huge hit in our house – they're like jam drops with drizzles of vanilla frosting. You could use apricot or plum jam instead, or use an assortment of flavours for variety in the cookie jar.

Makes 8 large cookies • Preparation 20 mins • Cook 1¼ hours • Cooker capacity 7 litres

1 cup plain (all-purpose) flour
½ cup caster (superfine) sugar
100 g (3½ oz) butter, melted
1 small egg, lightly beaten
½ teaspoon vanilla essence
¼ cup strawberry jam
Vanilla frosting, to decorate (see note)

1. Line the slow cooker with baking paper.

2. Combine the flour, sugar, butter, egg and vanilla in a mixing bowl. Stir to form a stiff dough.

3. Divide the mixture into 8 portions and roll into balls.

4. Place in the slow cooker, leaving plenty of space between balls to allow for spreading. Make an indentation in the centre of each ball with the back of a teaspoon, pressing only halfway through.

5. Fill each indentation with a teaspoon of jam.

6. Cover, putting a tea towel (dish towel) under the lid, and cook on high for 1¼ hours or until the cookies are semi-firm. They will become more firm as they cool.

7. Set aside on a rack to cool completely.

8. Drizzle the cookies with vanilla frosting.

NOTE: I use ready-made vanilla frosting that comes in a little pouch with a piping nozzle. You could of course make your own if you prefer not to buy it ready-made. A freezer bag with a corner snipped off makes a handy piping bag.

Two-Ingredient Cake

Could a cake be any easier? Vary the cake by varying the cake mix and the fruit – there are so many great pairings to be made. Vanilla and mango is one of my favourites; chocolate and cherry is another. Use the cake mix dry – don't mix it as per the packet instructions.

Serves 8–10 • Preparation 5 mins • Cook 1½–2 hours • Cooker capacity 1.5 litres

1 packet cake mix (see note)
425 g (15 oz) tinned fruit of your choice, in juice

1. Line the slow cooker with baking paper.
2. Combine the dry cake mix and the fruit and juice in a mixing bowl, and stir to combine. Pour the mixture into the slow cooker. (Alternatively, use a silicone cake pan in the slow cooker. If the bowl of your slow cooker is ceramic, pour water around the cake pan to a depth of about 1 cm (½ inch) to protect the bowl from cracking.)
3. Cover, putting a tea towel (dish towel) under the lid, and cook on high for 1½–2 hours, or until a skewer inserted into the cake comes out clean.
4. Remove the cake and set aside on a cooling rack.

NOTE: Choose whatever flavour of cake mix you like. The size of the packet isn't important – anything from 320 g (11 oz) to 440 g (1 lb) will work. Ice and decorate the cake as you wish, or enjoy it plain.

Baked Apples

This classic dessert is perfectly suited to slow cooking. You can change it up if you like by adding some sultanas or finely chopped mixed dried fruit to the filling.

Serves 4 • Preparation 10 mins • Cook 1 hour • Cooker capacity 6 litres

4 apples (I like to use Granny Smiths)
¼ cup brown sugar
1 teaspoon ground cinnamon
2 tablespoons butter
Vanilla ice cream, to serve

1. Core the apples and then peel a small strip around the top of each one to stop them from splitting during cooking. Place the apples in a slow cooker.

2. Combine the brown sugar and cinnamon in a small bowl. Fill the apple centres with the sugar mixture, pushing it in with a teaspoon until it's all used. Top each apple with 2 teaspoons butter.

3. Cover and cook on high for 1 hour.

4. Serve with vanilla ice cream.

Banana Pikelets

My kids love banana pikelets, but I don't like spending time standing by the stove to cook them the traditional way. I tried making them in silicone cupcake cases to prevent them from spreading too much in the slow cooker, and it worked great – the kids love these in their school lunchboxes! You'll need 30 silicone cupcake cases for this recipe or cook them in batches.

Makes 30 • Preparation 10 mins • Cook 45 mins • Cooker capacity 7 litres

2 cups self-raising flour, sifted
1½ cups milk
⅓ cup caster (superfine) sugar
2 eggs, lightly beaten
1½ tablespoons butter, melted
Pinch of salt
2 ripe bananas, mashed
Sliced banana and maple syrup or honey, to serve (optional)

1. Combine all the ingredients except the banana in a large bowl and mix well. Stir in the banana.

2. Divide the batter between 30 silicone cupcake cases – this means about 2 tablespoons of batter in each case, which will fill them about halfway. Transfer to the slow cooker.

3. Cover, putting a tea towel (dish towel) under the lid, and cook on high for 45 minutes, or until a skewer inserted in the middle of a pikelet comes out clean.

4. Serve with sliced banana and a drizzle of maple syrup or honey for breakfast, or just as they are in lunchboxes for a healthy snack.

Fudge

This recipe took the Slow Cooker Central Facebook group by storm in the lead-up to Christmas one year. Every second post for weeks and weeks was from someone cooking fudge. And everyone's fudge was totally different, because changing the type of chocolate and the flavourings and decorations changes the fudge. Using the basic method described here, the possibilities are endless. To inspire you, I've included some of my favourite variations, but feel free to experiment. Homemade slow-cooker fudge makes a great Christmas gift or a treat for the whole family.

Makes 40 small pieces • Preparation 5 mins • Cook 1½–2 hours • Cooker capacity 1.5 litres

> 500 g (1 lb 2 oz) chocolate, broken into chunks
> 1 tablespoon butter
> 1 tablespoon vanilla essence
> 395 g (14 oz) can sweetened condensed milk

1. Line a baking pan, about 20 cm x 20 cm (8 x 8 inches), with baking paper.

2. Combine all the ingredients in the slow cooker. Cook on low with the lid off for 1½–2 hours, stirring every 15 minutes or so with a silicone or metal spoon. Note it's very important that for fudge only, the lid stays OFF throughout cooking.

3. Pour into the prepared pan and place in the fridge to set (this takes at least 2 hours, but overnight is ideal).

4. Cut the fudge into squares and store in the fridge.

NOTE: To make Peanut Butter and Hazelnut Chocolate Fudge, replace the chocolate with 600 g (1 lb 5 oz) hazelnut chocolate, and add 3 tablespoons peanut butter with the other ingredients. Pour the cooked fudge into the pan, then heat an extra 2 tablespoons peanut butter in the microwave until runny. Drizzle the peanut butter over the fudge, and swirl it into the surface using a skewer.

White Chocolate Fudge is one of my favourites – I created it for a book-signing and fudge-tasting event when the first Slow Cooker Central book was published. Replace the chocolate with 600 g (1 lb 5 oz) white chocolate, and follow the basic method.

Peanut Butter & Oreo Brownies

I saw a recipe for brownies similar to these online and decided there must be a way to make them in the slow cooker. Using silicone muffin cases helps them to cook evenly, and makes each one the perfect portion size. There's no guarantee you'll be able to stop at just one 'portion' though! You'll need 16 silicone cupcake cases for this recipe.

Makes 16 • Preparation 20 mins • Cook 45 mins • Cooker capacity 7 litres

48 mini Oreo cookies (about 5 packets)
Peanut butter, for spreading
1 packet brownie mix, plus associated ingredients

1. Sandwich 3 mini Oreos together in a stack, spreading a generous amount of peanut butter between the layers and on top. Place each stack in a silicone cupcake case.

2. Prepare the brownie mix according to the packet instructions. I add an extra 1–2 tablespoons of water to make the mix easier to work with.

3. Divide the brownie mixture between the cupcake cases, spooning it around and on top of each Oreo stack.

4. Place the cupcake cases in the slow cooker. Cover, putting a tea towel (dish towel) under the lid, and cook on high for about 45 minutes or until the brownie mixture is set.

5. Cool on a wire rack, then remove the cases.

Banana Choc Chunk Muffins

I can hardly keep the fruit up to my little fruit-bat children (as I call them), but invariably we end up with a few over-ripe bananas here and there. This recipe is perfect to use them up and avoid waste!

Makes 12 • Preparation 15 mins • Cook 1 hour • Cooker capacity 7 litres

1½ cups wholemeal (or white) self-raising flour
½ cup caster (superfine) sugar
3 ripe bananas, mashed
⅓ cup milk
1 egg
1 tablespoon honey
100 g (3½ oz) milk chocolate chips

1. Combine the flour and sugar in a mixing bowl. Mix the banana, milk, egg and honey together, then stir into the dry ingredients. Fold the choc chips through.

2. Divide the mixture between 12 silicone muffin cases and place them in the slow cooker. If the bowl of your slow cooker is ceramic, pour water around the muffins to a depth of about 1 cm (½ inch) to protect the bowl from cracking.

3. Cover, putting a tea towel (dish towel) under the lid, and cook on high for 1 hour.

Bananas in Caramel Sauce

I made bananas in caramel sauce in the oven for years, but the recipe translates perfectly to the slow cooker. The result is caramelised bananas in the most decadent sauce. It's lovely served with creamy vanilla ice cream to balance the sweetness of the caramel.

Serves 4 • Preparation 5 mins • Cook 40 mins • Cooker capacity 7 litres

4 bananas, peeled and sliced lengthways
50 g (1¾ oz) butter
½ cup (lightly packed) light brown sugar
1 tablespoon apple juice

1. Line the slow cooker with baking paper and add the bananas, cut side down.

2. Melt the butter in a heatproof bowl in the microwave. Add the brown sugar and apple juice and stir to combine well. Pour the mixture over the bananas.

3. Cover, putting a tea towel (dish towel) under the lid, and cook on high for about 40 minutes, or until the banana is soft and the syrup is thick.

Fudge-tastic Brownies

I love slow-cooker fudge, and I love brownies. I wondered, could I unite my two loves in the one dish? The result – incredible decadent brownie bites with a sweet choc fudge topping. Yum!

I use a 7 litre cooker to make the base and a 1.5 litre cooker to make the fudge, but if you've only got one slow cooker, that's okay. Make the brownie base first, wash the slow cooker bowl, then start on the fudge. You may need to alter the cooking times to suit the size of your slow cooker. A larger cooker will cook the fudge much faster, and a smaller cooker may need longer to cook the brownie base all the way through.

Makes 40 small squares • Preparation 20 mins • Cook 1½ hours

BROWNIE BASE
2 cups caster (superfine) sugar
200 g (7 oz) butter, softened
1 cup plain (all-purpose) flour
½ cup cocoa powder
4 eggs, lightly beaten
1 teaspoon vanilla essence
½ teaspoon baking powder
½ teaspoon salt

FUDGE TOPPING
500g (1 lb 2 oz) milk chocolate, chopped
1 tablespoon butter
1 tablespoon vanilla essence
395 g (14 oz) can sweetened condensed milk

1. For the brownie base, line a 7 litre slow cooker with baking paper. Combine all the ingredients in a large mixing bowl and stir until smooth. Pour the mixture into the slow cooker. Cover, putting a tea towel (dish towel) under the lid, and cook on high 1 hour 20 minutes–1½ hours, or until a skewer inserted in the centre comes out clean.

2. Meanwhile, make the fudge topping. Combine all the ingredients in a 1.5 litre slow cooker. Cook on low with the lid off for 1½–2 hours, stirring every 15 minutes or so with a silicone or metal spoon.

3. To assemble, place the brownie base on a large tray. Pour the hot fudge over the base and smooth the top. Refrigerate to set for at least 4 hours or overnight.

4. Cut into pieces with a sharp knife and store in the refrigerator.

Chocolate Zucchini Cake

I was fascinated by the concept of using hidden vegetables in a cake. I was happy with the outcome of this recipe, and I assure you that won't be able to taste the zucchini. This cake is absolutely massive, so it's great value, and because it's full of vegetable we can fool ourselves that it's not too bad for us. After all, we all need another reason to eat cake – right?

Serves 20 • Preparation 15 mins • Cook 1 hour 50 mins • Cooker capacity 6 litres

Oil spray, for greasing
1 cup brown sugar
¾ cup caster (superfine) sugar
125 g (4½ oz) butter, softened
2⅓ cups self-raising flour
3 eggs, lightly beaten
¼ cup cocoa powder
1 teaspoon ground cinnamon
1 teaspoon vanilla essence
¼ teaspoon salt
3 cups grated zucchini
1 cup choc chips
½ cup Greek yoghurt

1. Spray the slow cooker lightly with oil and line it with baking paper.
2. Beat the sugars and butter in a large mixing bowl until creamy. Add the flour and eggs, stirring to combine well.
3. Add the cocoa, cinnamon, vanilla and salt. Stir to combine, then mix in the zucchini, choc chips and yoghurt. Stir until combined.
4. Pour the batter into the slow cooker.
5. Cover, putting a tea towel (dish towel) under the lid, and cook on high for 1 hour 50 minutes.

NOTE: Ice the cake if you desire, but I don't feel it needs it, as it's delicious without icing.

Apple Cinnamon Muffins

Imagine a doughnut dusted in cinnamon sugar, but without the hole. Add a hint of sweet apple and you have these apple cinnamon muffins. They're a huge hit with my kids, who love the sugary topping and the sweetness of the apple. And at less than $3.50 a batch to make, they won't break the bank. Great for lunchboxes and after-school treats. You'll need 20 silicone muffin cases for this recipe.

Makes 20 • Preparation 15 mins • Cook 40 mins • Cooker capacity 7 litres

MUFFINS
2½ cups self-raising flour
2 cups peeled and finely diced red apple
1 cup milk
⅔ cup caster (superfine) sugar
2 eggs, lightly beaten
50 g (1¾ oz) butter, softened
1 teaspoon ground cinnamon
½ teaspoon salt

CINNAMON SUGAR COATING
½ cup caster (superfine) sugar
1–2 teaspoons ground cinnamon
2–3 tablespoons butter, melted

1. To make the muffins, combine all the ingredients in a large mixing bowl and mix well. Divide the mixture between 20 silicone muffin cases.

2. Place the muffins in the slow cooker. If the bowl of your slow cooker is ceramic, pour water around the cases to a depth of about 1 cm (½ inch) to protect the bowl from cracking.

3. Cover, putting a tea towel (dish towel) under the lid, and cook on high for 40 minutes, or until a skewer inserted in the centre of a muffin comes out clean.

4. Transfer to a wire rack until just cool enough to handle. Remove the muffins from the cases.

5. For the coating, mix the sugar and cinnamon in a small bowl. Dip the muffins top-down into the butter, allowing the excess to drip off. Press them into the sugar mixture to coat.

Peanut Butter Choc Chunk Cookies

There's something about peanut butter and chocolate that makes them so good together, especially in a cookie. Based on simple ingredients that you probably have on hand, these are a breeze to make and a delight to eat.

Makes 20 • Preparation 10 mins • Cook 1 hour • Cooker capacity 7 litres

1 cup caster (superfine) sugar
1 cup peanut butter (I use crunchy)
1 egg
1 teaspoon vanilla essence
½ cup choc chips

1. Combine the sugar, peanut butter, egg and vanilla in a mixing bowl and mix well. Add the choc chips and mix until combined.

2. Line the slow cooker with baking paper. Roll the dough into balls about the size of a golf ball. Place them in the slow cooker, spaced well apart, and press with a fork to flatten (I cook 8 per batch in my 7 litre rectangular slow cooker).

3. Cover, putting a tea towel (dish towel) under the lid, and cook on high for 1 hour. Repeat with remaining dough.

4. Enjoy hot, or allow to cool and store in a sealed container.

BREADS, DIPS AND SAUCES

Cheesy Bacon and Relish Focaccia

This focaccia is VERY heavy on the toppings, delivering a ratio of bread to bacon and cheese that means every bite is packed with flavour. It will have you drooling. So good!

Serves 10 • Preparation 25 mins • Cook 1¾ hours • Cooker capacity 7 litres

Oil spray, for greasing
3 cups self-raising flour
2 cups warm water
Pinch of salt
300 g (10½ oz) diced bacon
250 g (9 oz) jar tomato relish
2 cups grated tasty cheese

1. Line the slow cooker with baking paper and spray it with oil.

2. Combine the flour, water and salt in a large bowl and mix to form a sticky dough. Add half the cheese and half the bacon and mix well.

3. Spread the dough into the slow cooker and top with the tomato relish. Scatter with the remaining bacon, then the remaining cheese.

4. Cover, putting a tea towel (dish towel) under the lid, and cook on high for 1¾ hours or until cooked through.

Loaded Cheese & Bacon Cob Loaf Pull-Apart

Who doesn't love a cob loaf or pull-apart bread at a party? There are so many options for fillings. I chose cheese and bacon for this one because – well, cheese and bacon are meant to be. Turn up to a party with this bad boy and you'll be the talk of the night!

Serves 10 • Preparation 20 mins • Cook 2 hours • Cooker capacity 7 litres

450 g (1 lb) crusty cob loaf
125 g (4½ oz) butter
200 g (7 oz) diced bacon
1 onion, diced
2–4 garlic cloves, minced
½ cup thinly sliced spring onions (scallions)
230 g (8 oz) grated tasty cheese

1. Make five deep cuts across the top of the cob loaf, but don't slice all the way through. Rotate the loaf 90 degrees and make three more cuts. You should have a checkerboard pattern of cuts.

2. Heat 25 g (1 oz) of the butter in a small frying pan over medium heat. Add the bacon, onion and garlic and cook for 5–10 minutes, until the onion is translucent and the bacon is lightly cooked. Transfer to a bowl and stir in the spring onion and 130 g (4½ oz) of the grated cheese.

3. Take two long sheets of aluminium foil (about 60 cm/2 ft each) and lay one on top of the other at 90 degrees so they form an X shape. Place the cob loaf in the middle.

4. Carefully spoon the bacon mixture into the cuts in the loaf. Melt the remaining butter and pour it over the loaf and into the cuts. Top with the remaining grated cheese.

5. Wrap the loaf securely in the foil and place it in the slow cooker.

6. Cover and cook on high for 2 hours.

7. Unwrap the loaf carefully, as it will be hot, then serve.

NOTE: If you like, you can brown the loaf (without the foil) on a tray in a preheated oven for a few minutes before serving.

Cob-less Hot Cob Dip

Think of a lush cob loaf – minus the cob! Enjoy this hot dip right from the serving bowl. Our kids love to tuck into this at parties with carrot, cucumber and celery sticks, bread sticks, or tortilla chips. It's great for low-carb folk, for parties and for entertaining. A cheesy, creamy dip delight!

Serves 10 • Preparation 15 mins • Cook 1¾ hours • Cooker capacity 6 litres

250 g (9 oz) block cream cheese, chopped
⅔ cup cooking cream
⅔ cup sour cream
150 g (5½ oz) diced bacon
1 cup grated tasty cheese
40 g (1½ oz) packet French onion soup mix
⅔ cup grated mozzarella cheese
¼ cup chopped fresh chives

1. Lay a sheet of baking paper on the base of the slow cooker bowl (just to protect the surface). Place a suitably sized heatproof serving dish in the slow cooker. Pour water around the dish to a depth of about 2 cm (¾ inch).

2. Combine the cream cheese, cream, sour cream, bacon, tasty cheese and soup mix in a mixing bowl. Mix well, then transfer to the serving dish.

3. Cover, putting a tea towel (dish towel) under the lid, and cook on high for 1½ hours, stirring once during the cooking time.

4. Sprinkle the top with the mozzarella cheese and chives, cover (replace the tea towel) and cook for a further 15 minutes.

5. Carefully remove the dish from the slow cooker. Wipe the water from the bottom of the dish then serve straight to the table.

NOTE: I use an ovenproof ceramic dish about 23 cm (9 inches) long, 15 cm (6 inches) wide and 7cm (2¾ inches) deep.

Creamy Mushroom Sauce

I love the convenience of a slow-cooked sauce. Even if you're busy barbecuing or pan-frying meat, you can relax knowing that your sauce is simmering away ready to serve. This lush creamy mushroom version is perfect on steaks and chicken fillets too.

Serves 4 • Preparation 15 mins • Cook 2 hours • Cooker capacity 1.5 litres

300 ml (10 fl oz) cooking cream
3 teaspoons beef stock powder
2 cups sliced button mushrooms
1 tablespoon cornflour (cornstarch), mixed to a slurry with 1 tablespoon water

1. Combine the cream and stock in the slow cooker. Stir in the mushrooms.

2. Cover and cook on high for 1¾ hours.

3. Stir in the cornflour slurry and cook for 15 minutes or until thickened.

▬— Cheese and Mustard Sauce —●

Slow cookers LOVE corned beef! (See the recipes on page 183.) So we needed a perfect slow-cooked sauce to accompany that classic dish. This cheesy sauce with a touch of mustard is just the thing.

Serves 6 • Preparation 10 mins • Cook 1½ hours • Cooker capacity 1.5 litres

2 cups full-cream (whole) milk
2 tablespoons cornflour (cornstarch)
1 cup grated tasty cheese
1 heaped tablespoon wholegrain mustard
2 teaspoons mustard powder
½ teaspoon salt

1. Whisk the milk and cornflour together until smooth. Pour into the slow cooker. Stir in the remaining ingredients.

2. Cover and cook on high for 1½ hours, whisking occasionally to prevent lumps and sticking.

3. Serve hot.

INDEX

1–2–3 roast beef 179

A
absorbent pads from meat trays
    13–14
apples
  apple cinnamon muffins 270
  apple crumble 253
  baked apples 262
apricot chicken three ways 131
Asian-inspired whole chicken 92
asparagus
  quiche, chicken and asparagus 118
  roast beef dinner, complete 173
Aussie lamb shanks 101
auto function 9

B
bacon
  beans and bacon breakfast mugs
    with eggs 241
  brisket, bacon and barbecue 169
  Brussels sprouts with bacon 74
  burgers, barbecue bacon 235
  cauliflower bake, loaded 55
  chicken, smoky barbecue, with
    bacon 133
  chicken, smoky maple and
    barbecue hasselback 117
  cob loaf pull-apart, loaded cheese
    and bacon 276
  dip, cob-less hot cob 277
  focaccia, cheesy bacon and relish
    275
  morning mushrooms 246
  pasta, cheesy one pot sausage and
    veggie 50

pigs in blankets 205
  potato bake with chorizo and
    bacon, creamy 72
  quiche squares, quick and easy
    245
  soup, easy pea and ham 36
baked beans
  beans and bacon breakfast mugs
    with eggs 241
  barbecue bacon burgers 235
bananas
  cake, hummingbird, with cream
    cheese frosting 256
  in caramel sauce 267
  muffins, banana choc chunk 266
  pear and banana muffins 255
  pikelets, banana 263
beans, canned
  burgers, barbecue bacon 235
  mince and potato bake, Mexican
    220
  nachos, beef 222
  shredded beef, must try Mexican
    88
  soup, minestrone 32
beans, raw red kidney, safety
    concerns and 21–22
beef
  bake, Mexican mince and potato
    220
  beef and black bean 84
  brisket, bacon and barbecue 169
  brisket, saucy shredded 171
  burgers, barbecue bacon 235
  casserole, beef and red wine 177
  casserole, Mexican potato gem 225
  chow mein, easy 96

corned beef 183
cottage pie 227
curry, family friendly beef 181
hamburger helpers 221
hot pot 170
Hungarian beef goulash 172
meatloaves, glazed mini 217
mince, classic curried 229
mince, rich gravy 232
mince, savoury 226
mince, slow cooked Mexican taco 91
nachos, beef 222
pasta, creamy beef and 218
porcupines in barbecue sauce 228
ribs, sticky steakhouse 182
'roast' beef 175
roast beef, 1–2–3 179
roast beef dinner, complete 173
roast beef with rich gravy 176
Salisbury steak 223
shredded beef, must try Mexican 88
spaghetti and meatballs, meatlover's 43
spaghetti bolognese 49
steak, nanny's braised 180
strips in sweet soy sauce 178
teriyaki beef 87
biscuits
peanut butter choc chunk cookies 271
strawberries and cream cookies 260
blueberry pancake slab 258
bolognese, spaghetti 49
bread trick 8
brisket, bacon and barbecue 169
brisket, saucy shredded 171

broccoli
beef and black bean 84
and cauliflower bake, cheesy 73
and cauliflower stuffed potatoes, cheesy 70
sweet chilli butter 64
brownies
double choc fudge 257
fudge-tastic 268
peanut butter and Oreo 265
Brussels sprouts
with bacon 74
roast beef dinner, complete 173
burgers, barbecue bacon 235
buttermilk cabbage 62

C

cabbage
buttermilk 62
chow mein, easy 96
cakes
blueberry pancake slab 258
brownies, double choc fudge 257
brownies, fudge-tastic 268
brownies, peanut butter and Oreo 265
carrot 252
chocolate zucchini 269
cinnamon, with cinnamon butter glaze 251
hummingbird, with cream cheese frosting 256
strawberry and sultana scrolls, sweet 259
techniques for slow cooking 22–23
two-ingredient 261
calamari
seafood marinara fettuccine 192
seafood medley, creamy garlic 191

caramel sauce, bananas in 267

carrots

carrot cake 252

carrot and parsnip purée 57

carrot soup, curried 35

casserole, rustic lamb 108

honey carrots 69

one pot dinner, roast vegetable, sausage and gravy 155

roast beef dinner, complete 173

sausages, curried 162

cauliflower

cauliflower bake, cheesy broccoli and 73

cauliflower bake, loaded 55

cauliflower, whole, with Moroccan butter seasoning 58

potatoes, cheesy broccoli and cauliflower stuffed 70

ceramic slow cooker bowls 5

char siu style roast pork 201

cheese

beef nachos 222

burgers, barbecue bacon 235

casserole, Mexican potato gem 225

cauliflower bake, loaded 55

cheese and mustard sauce 279

cheese and salami sticks 212

chicken, barbecue shredded cheesy 126

chicken, cheesy salami 140

chicken made easy, creamy garlic 141

chicken parmigiana, naked 148

chicken, pizza 124

chicken, smoky maple and barbecue hasselback 117

cottage pie 227

dip, cob-less hot cob 277

eggs, beans and bacon breakfast mugs with 241

focaccia, cheesy bacon and relish 275

ham steaks, Hawaiian 202

hamburger helpers 221

mince and potato bake, Mexican 220

mushrooms, morning 246

nachos, beef 222

pasta bake, creamy, cheesy chicken and tomato 46

pasta, cheesy one pot sausage and veggie 50

pasta, one pot chicken alfredo 48

pie, chicken potato 233

pie, cottage 227

pie, shepherd's 227

pizza cups, mini muffin 224

potato bake with chorizo and bacon, creamy 72

potato smash, cheesy 67

potatoes, cheesy broccoli and cauliflower stuffed 70

pull-apart, loaded cheese and bacon cob loaf 276

quiche, chicken and asparagus 118

quiche, crustless crab 194

ravioli, cheesy chicken and chorizo 47

sauce, cheese and mustard 279

shepherd's pie 227

sticks, cheese and salami 212

sweet potato bake 65

chicken

apricot chicken three ways 131

barbecue plum 139

barbecue shredded cheesy 126

cacciatore 121

carbonara chicken meatballs 236
  cheesy salami 140
  creamy garlic, made easy 141
  creamy Mexican 137
  cup-a-laksa, creamy chicken 145
  curry, chutney chicken 128
  curry, mild Thai chicken and mango
    85
  curry, Thai chicken and prawn
    yellow 93
  curry, Thai green chicken 94
  French cream, with four ingredients
    143
  fricassee 136
  hasselback, smoky maple and
    barbecue 117
  honey and garlic 147
  honey balsamic 138
  honey mustard 134
  laksa 81
  lemon 120
  mango chutney drumsticks 125
  marsala 119
  mee goreng 79
  memory lane 130
  mustard maple 142
  naked parmigiana 148
  pasta, one pot alfredo 48
  pasta bake, creamy, cheesy chicken
    and tomato 46
  pizza chicken 124
  pizza cups, mini muffin 224
  poached breast 144
  poached breast with garlic,
    Moroccan 123
  potato pie 233
  quiche, chicken and asparagus 118
  quiches, chicken and corn mini
    244

  ravioli, cheesy chicken and chorizo
    47
  Singapore noodles with chicken,
    prawns and Chinese barbecue
    pork 82
  smoky barbecue, with bacon 133
  soup, Chinese chicken noodle and
    sweet corn 33
  soup, super easy 37
  Spanish 95
  Spanish bake, loaded 90
  sticky teriyaki 135
  stock, homemade 31
  supercharged satay 122
  sweet chilli barbecue 114
  sweet soy Asian 146
  taco chicken 113
  Thai peanut 89
  tikka masala, super simple 83
  tomato and pesto pasta 44
  tomato and spinach drumsticks,
    creamy 127
  tomato pesto 129
  tropical 116
  whole, Asian-inspired 92
  whole, honey barbecue 132
  whole, shredded, garlic butter and
    white wine 115
  whole, techniques for slow cooking
    12–13
chocolate
  brownies, double choc fudge 257
  brownies, fudge-tastic 268
  brownies, peanut butter and Oreo
    265
  cake, chocolate zucchini 269
  cookies, peanut butter choc chunk
    271
  muffins, banana choc chunk 266

chorizo
  bake, creamy potato with chorizo
    and bacon 72
  bake, loaded Spanish 90
  pasta, creamy beef and 218
  ravioli, cheesy chicken and chorizo
    47
  Spanish chicken 95
chow mein, easy 96
cinnamon cake with cinnamon butter
    glaze 251
citrus corned beef 183
cleaning slow cookers 17–19
cob-less hot cob dip 277
cob loaf pull-apart, loaded cheese and
    bacon 276
coconut
  curry, family friendly beef 181
  sausages, mango coconut curry
    160
  vegetables, coconut curry 60
converting recipes for slow cooking
    26–27
cookies
  peanut butter choc chunk cookies
    271
  strawberries and cream cookies
    260
corn
  corn cobs, honey mustard 71
  Mexican sausages 80
  quiches, chicken and corn mini
    194, 244, 245
  quiche squares, quick and easy
    245
  soup, Chinese chicken noodle and
    sweet corn 33
corned beef 183
cornflour as thickener 5–6

cottage pie 227
crab quiche, crustless 194
cream cheese frosting 256
cream, slow cooking with 15–16
crumbed fish cakes 189
curries
  beef curry, family friendly 181
  chicken curry, Thai green 94
  chicken and mango curry, mild Thai
    85
  chicken and prawn yellow curry,
    Thai 93
  chicken laksa 81
  chicken tikka masala, super simple
    83
  chutney chicken curry 128
  coconut curry vegetables 60
  lamb curry, sweet 104
  mince, classic curried 229
  prawns, curried 187
  sausage curry, sweet 164
  sausages, curried 162
  sausages, mango coconut curry 160

D
dairy products, slow cooking with
    15–16
desserts
  apple crumble 253
  baked apples 262
  bananas in caramel sauce 267
  raisin bread and butter pudding 254
diet recipes for slow cookers 20–21
dip, cob-less hot cob 277

E
eggs
  beans and bacon breakfast mugs
    with eggs 241

chow mein, easy 96
omelette, no fail filled 242
quiche squares, quick and easy
    245
quiche, chicken and asparagus 118
quiche, crustless crab 194
quiches, chicken and corn mini 244
Singapore noodles with chicken,
    prawns and Chinese barbecue
    pork 82

F
fat and oil, removing from slow cooked
    dishes 8
fish
    fettuccine, seafood marinara 192
    fillets, Asian inspired 188
    fillets, Mediterranean 190
    fish cakes, crumbed 189
    seafood medley, creamy garlic 191
focaccia, cheesy bacon and relish
    275
food safety. See safety and slow
    cooking
frozen meat, safety concerns about
    4–5
fudge 264
    brownies, fudge-tastic 268
    techniques for slow cooking 23–25

G
garlic butter hasselback potatoes 61
garlic butter mushrooms 68
ginger beer corned beef 183
gravy granules as thickener 6

H
ham steaks, Hawaiian 202
hamburger helpers 221

hasselback chicken, smoky maple and
    barbecue 117
hasselback potatoes, garlic butter 61
hasselback sweet potatoes 59
Hawaiian ham steaks 202
Hungarian beef goulash 172

I
ice-cube trick 8
Italian meatball subs 230

K
kidney beans, safety concerns and
    21–22

L
lamb
    casserole, rustic 108
    curry, sweet 104
    meatballs with minted yoghurt
        dressing 107
    obsession 103
    roast lamb and gravy rolls 102
    roast, with rosemary butter and red
        wine sauce 109
    shanks, Aussie 101
    shepherd's pie 227
    sliders, saucy pulled lamb and slaw
        106
lemon chicken 120
lemonade corned beef 183

M
mangoes
    chicken drumsticks, mango chutney
        125
    curry, mild Thai chicken and mango
        85
    sausages, mango coconut curry 160

meat, pre-browning 11
meatballs
    carbonara chicken 236
    and gravy, easy 234
    lamb, with minted yoghurt dressing 107
    porcupines in barbecue sauce 228
    Salisbury steak 223
    spaghetti and, meatlover's 43
    subs, Italian 230
    turkey 231
meat, frozen, safety concerns about 4–5
meatloaves, glazed mini 217
mee goreng 79
memory lane chicken 130
Mexican chicken, creamy 137
Mexican mince and potato bake 220
Mexican potato gem casserole 225
Mexican pulled pork sliders 209
Mexican sausages 80
Mexican shredded beef, must try 88
Mexican taco mince, slow cooked 91
minestrone soup 32
mint peas 56
muffins
    apple cinnamon 270
    banana choc chunk 266
    pear and banana 255
mushrooms
    beef and red wine casserole 177
    chicken cacciatore 121
    chicken fricassee 136
    chicken marsala 119
    garlic butter 68
    hamburger helpers 221
    morning mushrooms 246
    mushroom sauce, creamy 278
    mushroom sausages 158

quiche squares, quick and easy 245
    Salisbury steak 223
mussels
    seafood marinara fettuccine 192
    seafood medley, creamy garlic 191

N
nachos, beef 222
nanny's braised steak 180
noodles
    chicken laksa 81
    chow mein, easy 96
    mee goreng 79
    Singapore noodles with chicken,prawns and Chinese barbecue pork 82
    soup, Chinese chicken noodle and sweet corn 33

O
oats
    apple crumble 253
    porridge, fast and warming 243
oil, removing from slow cooked dishes 8
olives
    chicken cacciatore 121
    Spanish chicken 95
omelette, no fail filled 242
oven conversion times and slow cooking 26–27

P
pantry staples 25
parsnip purée, carrot and 57
pasta
    chicken alfredo, one pot 48
    chicken and tomato pasta bake, creamy, cheesy 46

creamy beef and 218
ravioli, cheesy chicken and chorizo
    47
sausage and veggie, cheesy one
    pot 50
seafood marinara fettuccine 192
spaghetti and meatballs, meatlover's
    43
spaghetti bolognese 49
techniques for slow cooking 16–17
tomato and pesto chicken 44
tomato pasta sauce, homemade 45
pea and ham soup, easy 36
peanut butter
brownies, peanut butter and Oreo
    265
cookies, peanut butter choc chunk
    271
satay chicken, supercharged 122
satay sausages, creamy 163
Thai peanut chicken 89
pear and banana muffins 255
peas
curried sausages 162
lamb casserole, rustic 108
mint peas 56
pesto
chicken and tomato pasta bake,
    creamy, cheesy 46
Mediterranean fish fillets 190
tomato and pesto chicken pasta 44
tomato pesto chicken 129
pies
chicken potato 233
cottage 227
shepherd's 227
pigs in blankets 205
pikelets, banana 263
pineapple

cake, hummingbird, with cream
    cheese frosting 256
chicken, tropical 116
ham steaks, Hawaiian 202
pork mince, sweet and sour 219
pork rashers, sweet and sour 210
pizza chicken 124
pizza cups, mini muffin 224
porcupines in barbecue sauce 228
pork
char siu style roast 201
chops, creamy pepper 211
chops, simple 'n' saucy 207
chops, sweet chilli 208
fillet, sweet barbecue-style 200
meatball subs, Italian 230
meatballs and gravy, easy 234
mince, sweet and sour 219
rashers, sweet and sour 210
ribs, barbecue plum 203
ribs, honey soy and garlic 199
san choy bow 86
saucy pulled 206
Singapore noodles with
    chicken,prawns and Chinese
    barbecue pork 82
sliders, Mexican pulled pork 209
spaghetti and meatballs, meatlover's
    43
steaks in pepper sauce 204
porridge, fast and warming 243
potato as thickener 6
potatoes
bake, creamy potato, with chorizo
    and bacon 72
bake, Mexican mince and potato
    220
bake, Spanish loaded 90
baked baby 59, 61, 63, 70, 75

beef hot pot 170

casserole, Mexican potato gem 225

cheesy broccoli and cauliflower
    stuffed 70

fish cakes, crumbed 189

garlic butter hasselback 61

honey mustard 63

lamb casserole, rustic 108

one pot dinner, roast vegetable,
    sausage and gravy 155

pie, chicken potato 233

pie, cottage 227

pie, shepherd's 227

roast beef dinner, complete 173

sausages, curried 162

smash, cheesy 67

vegetables, coconut curry 60

prawns

    curried 187

    curry, Thai chicken and prawn
        yellow 93

    seafood marinara fettuccine 192

    seafood medley, creamy garlic 191

    Singapore noodles with chicken,
        prawns and Chinese barbecue
        pork 82

pudding, raisin bread and butter 254

pull-apart, loaded cheese and bacon
    cob loaf 276

pumpkin

    lamb casserole, rustic 108

    one pot dinner, roast vegetable,
        sausage and gravy 155

    roast beef dinner, complete 173

    soup, classic creamy 38

Q

quiche

    chicken and asparagus 118

chicken and corn mini 244

crab, crustless 194

squares, quick and easy 245

R

ravioli, cheesy chicken and chorizo 47

recipes, converting, for slow cooking
        26–27

red kidney beans, safety concerns and
        21–22

'roast' beef 175

roast beef, 1–2–3 179

roast beef dinner, complete 173

roast beef with rich gravy 176

rolls, subs and sliders

    burgers, barbecue bacon 235

    hamburger helpers 221

    meatball subs, Italian 230

    rolls, roast lamb and gravy 102

    sliders, Mexican pulled pork 209

    sliders, saucy pulled lamb and slaw
        106

S

safety and slow cookers

    absorbent pads from meat trays
        13–14

    frozen meat 4–5

    raw red kidney beans 21–22

    tea towel trick 7

    timers 9

    unattended cooking 10

salami

    cheese and salami sticks 212

    cheesy salami chicken 140

Salisbury steak 223

san choy bow 86

satay chicken, supercharged 122

satay sausages, creamy 163

sausages
    apricot chicken three ways 131
    in barbecue and mustard sauce 161
    chicken stroganoff sausages 157
    chutney and tomato sausages 159
    creamy satay 163
    curried 162
    curry, sweet sausage 164
    devilled 156
    mango coconut curry 160
    Mexican 80
    mushroom sausages 158
    one pot dinner, roast vegetable,
        sausage and gravy 155
    pasta, cheesy one pot sausage and
        veggie 50
    pigs in blankets 205
    sweet chilli 154
    sweet sauce sausages 153
savoury mince 226
scallops, lemon and garlic butter 193
scrolls, sweet strawberry and sultana
    259
seafood marinara mix
    seafood marinara fettuccine 192
    seafood medley, creamy garlic 191
seasonal slow cooking 19–20
shepherd's pie 227
silverside 183. *See also* corned beef
Singapore noodles with
        chicken,prawns and Chinese
        barbecue pork 82
sliders
    Mexican pulled pork 209
    saucy pulled lamb and slaw 106
soups
    carrot, curried 35
    chicken noodle and sweet corn,
        Chinese 33

chicken stock, homemade 31
chicken, super easy 37
minestrone 32
pea and ham, easy 36
pumpkin, classic creamy 38
tomato, zesty 34
spaghetti and meatballs, meatlover's
    43
spaghetti bolognese 49
Spanish bake, loaded 90
Spanish chicken 95
steak, nanny's braised 180
stock, homemade chicken 31
subs, Italian meatball 230
summer slow cooking 19–20
sweet potatoes
    coconut curry vegetables 60
    hasselback 59
    one pot dinner, roast vegetable,
        sausage and gravy 155
    roast beef dinner, complete 173
    sweet potato bake 65

T
taco chicken 113
taco mince, slow cooked Mexican 91
tea towel trick 6, 7
teriyaki beef 87
teriyaki chicken, sticky 135
Thai chicken and prawn yellow curry
    93
Thai green chicken curry 94
Thai peanut chicken 89
thickening slow cooked dishes 5–7
timers and slow cooking 9
tomatoes
    bake, loaded Spanish 90
    beef goulash, Hungarian 172
    beef nachos 222

beef and pasta, pasta 218

  beef and red wine casserole 177

  chicken cacciatore 121

  chicken drumsticks, creamy tomato
    and spinach 127

  chicken, Spanish 95

  chicken tomato pesto 129

  fish fillets, Mediterranean 190

  meatball subs, Italian 230

  mushrooms, morning 246

  nachos, beef, 222

  pasta sauce, homemade 45

  pasta, cheesy one pot sausage and
    veggie 50

  pasta, tomato and pesto chicken
    44

  porcupines in barbecue sauce 228

  potato gem casserole, Mexican 225

  ravioli, cheesy chicken and chorizo
    47

  sausages, chutney and tomato 159

  sausages, Mexican 80

  seafood marinara fettuccine 192

  sliders, Mexican pulled pork 209

  soup, minestrone 32

  soup, zesty 34

  spaghetti and meatballs, meatlover's
    43

tropical chicken 116

tuna fish cakes, crumbed 189

turkey meatballs 231

two-ingredient cake 261

V

veal

  meatballs and gravy, easy 234

  meatball subs, Italian 230

vegetables, basic, slow-cooked style
  66

vegetables, coconut curry 60

W

weight loss and slow cooking 20–21

Z

zucchini cake, chocolate 269

THANK YOU

Thank you to my amazing admin team who help me run our Facebook group 'Slow Cooker Recipes 4 Families' each and every day.

Felicity, Karen, Denise, Nikki, Victoria and Simon – I could never keep up were it not for your help, and I am forever grateful for all that you do xx

As always my eternal admiration, respect and thanks go to Brigitta Doyle, Publishing Director of HarperCollins. You came into my world completely unexpected on that fateful day years ago. You gave me a new path in life I'd never even dreamed of! Your faith in me and faith in our shared goals drives me to always do my very best and the results we achieve have been nothing short of astounding. You are, and always will be the woman who changed my life x

Thank you also to Lachlan McLaine, Matthew Howard and all the incredible team at ABC Books and HarperCollins Australia. I am so blessed to work with such an accomplished team of professionals who guide and support my every step from conception to publication and beyond.

Special thanks to my dear friend Toni McCulloch of Master of Coin & Cloud Accounting Maroochydore. Besides your amazing & professional accounting work, on a personal level also, you are an incredible wealth of moral and spiritual support and I cannot thank you enough for always being the voice of serenity when I need you.

To my Dad, Marty, and my big sisters Vicki and Debbie, I hope I continue to make you proud and I hope that somewhere out there our Mum is watching down on me and feeling the same xx

To those friends who understand the pressures always upon me, the engagements I miss or the social times I still must pull out my phone to work at, even when everyone else is having time off – thank you

To my amazing husband Simon and our beautiful children who champion my every cause, who share my every success, who celebrate my every step along this journey – I couldn't do this without you.

I am so eternally grateful to share this journey with you, to share this life with you. For you I will always strive to do my best, to be the best me that I can be and together to live our best life always.

I love you all to the moon and back again!

I hope to always make you proud, as I am so proud of you all!

You are my world xx

Last but not least, thank you to each and every member of our online community!

We may have over half a million Facebook members and millions more website members, but every single individual is part of who we are.

We share our recipes, we share our successes and our occasional funny fails, we share our great meal moments and our creative meal moments and we share our knowledge. We share our every days and together, that makes us what we are … our amazing online Slow Cooker Central slow-cooking community.

YOU are the reason I do what I do. YOU are so often the first people I speak to every day and the last people I speak to every night, and all day in between.

We have created something so special together … and YOU are what makes that special.

So THANK YOU. Xx

Slow-cooking internet sensation Paulene Christie is a busy working mum with a passion for sharing new and exciting recipes for the slow cooker. She now has more than 550,000 members in her Facebook group, Slow Cooker Recipes 4 Families, and a hugely successful website, Slow Cooker Central. The Facebook page is so popular that Paulene has a team of six people (including her husband, Simon) to help her administer the thousands of recipes and comments that are posted each day. Paulene lives in Queensland with Simon, their three young children and 30 slow cookers.

www.slowcookercentral.com
www.facebook.com/groups/SlowCookerRecipes4Families